THE

FELLOWSHIP OF GHOSTS

A Guide To Overcoming

Walter Justice

Walter Justice, PO Box 8932, Boise ID 83707

This book is dedicated to Yvonne, my grandma.
A true servant of God who gave me some
of the most wonderful days of my life.

Yvonne Augusta Curran/Borgardt
April 28th, 1914 -- October 24th, 2008

Table of Contents

PROLOGUE

Ever since I was a little boy, I was taught about the armor of God. [Ephesians 6:11-17] I marched to catchy Sunday school songs, and pretended I was a soldier in God's army. As I grew older, I listened to ministers preach on the Ephesians text. They gave the history and purpose of each piece of armor, and then drew comparisons and analogies to biblical doctrines and principles. If I recall correctly, Roman soldiers soaked their shields in water. Later, as a battle waged, the fiery arrows of the enemy fizzled as they struck the drenched Roman shields. In turn, the apostle Paul tells us,

> *...take up the shield of faith, with which you can extinguish all the flaming arrows of the evil one.* [Ephesians 6:16]

For the believer, our faith is in Jesus Christ, and "soaked" in the word of God.

The spiritual warfare movement evolved over the last couple of decades. Many believers embraced a warfare, or good versus evil paradigm. People from all walks of life, including Christians, have a tendency to polarize any newly found truth. An individual truth can become the end-all, overshadowing all others. After I came to an experiential understanding of the powers of evil, I saw virtually everything through that grid. I slid into hyper-spirituality.

While married to my first wife, demons manifested

in our house. I felt like I was living through a creepy movie. On one or two occasions, after my ex-wife saw a giant spider crawling on the wall, she had welts or bites on her leg. Another time, she saw a figure like a snowman on our bed, and then the figure disappeared. I froze throughout that night. We were living in central California. The summers sizzled, and even the nights exceeded 90 degrees Fahrenheit. I rolled over in bed and saw a black, spindly hand hovering over my ex-wife's head. The index finger rested on her forehead. Once again, like the other creatures, the hand quickly disappeared. When my ex-wife woke up the following day, she had such a severe migraine, she vomited throughout the morning. We listened to Christian tapes when we went to bed too. One evening, I put a tape in and pushed play. Immediately the deck clicked off. I pushed play again, and once again, the deck clicked off. It happened a third time. I finally said, "In the name of Jesus I bind you." Then the tape played.

A gracious, little old lady ministered to us during this season. She felt there was something in the ground. Our battle quickly came to a climax. My ex-wife and I were praying in bed. She saw two arrow heads butted up against each other floating in our room. She told me the arrowheads moved toward the bedroom door. I immediately got up, ran for the door, and slammed it shut. Like a door is going to stop demons! They were gone.

We lived near a river where some local tribes used to stay during the winter months. When the weather warmed up, they migrated to the mountains. Apparently something occurred on our property, or in our neighborhood. I anointed the four corners of our property with oil, declared ownership, and told any and all foul spirits to leave our property and neighborhood, "in the name of Jesus." There was an immediate shift. We were no longer harassed by demons in our house. Also, our neighbors across the street partied with other neighbors almost every weekend. The families fought, and the weekend binges abruptly ended. A gentle peace came over our home and neighborhood.

After my initial immersion in spiritual warfare, I chased demons everywhere. I was polarized. Every difficult situation or event was caused by our adversary the devil. I and other spiritual warriors violently rebuked powers and principalities. I ministered deliverance all the time too. Even with extremism, many people were healed and delivered.

Yet, for all the prayers and fasting we did, communities remained unchanged. A number of individuals continued to be plagued by the same issues. I couldn't even seem to win a few of my own battles. Wasn't Jesus greater than the devil? Why wasn't I overcoming? Something was seriously wrong. My warfare paradigm no longer worked for me. Eventually my life completely fell apart. Two marriages crumbled, and I lost a child, a home, friends, and even my health. I lived through abuse and rejection. Nevertheless, my gracious God was in the whole thing. The problem was me. He exposed the wickedness of my heart.

Not too long ago, God finished a deep healing in my heart. I felt the beginnings of this transformation over the last couple of years. I consistently saw an arrow traveling through water. The arrow traveled fast, but slowed down and stopped because of the resistance of the water. The Lord revealed to me that the water was symbolic of me. Issues and struggles which held sway over me no longer did. Darkness, like the arrow, passed through; yet, there was still enough of Walter that I slowed down the passing darkness. Then, God completed a work in my heart. I now envision an arrow whistling through the air; it just keeps on going. I'm more like air than water these days. Or, I'm more ghostlike. Stuff just passes through me. Here's what God did. The "finishing" started with a strange, but vivid dream.

Dream: I am walking through a community. On each side of me are stores. A few cars are parked in the street. It's dark, and street lights illuminate the road and the stores. I don't see any other people. Maybe it was the wee hours of the morning. I walk in the street, but off to the left side a little bit. In my left hand, I'm holding the hand of my paternal grandfather, and in my right hand I'm holding a branding iron with the initials of my maternal grandfather. I never knew my maternal grandfather; he was killed in a train accident before I was born. I let go of my paternal grandfather's hand, and he was gone. I continue walking for the longest time, still holding the branding iron. Off in the distance, almost as if he's in an alley-way or side street, I see my grandfather. I take up his hand again, and continue on my journey. **End of dream.**

Before I married my first wife, I played hard, I partied. When I married, I decided I was no longer responsible just for myself, but also for another person. I shut down the partying. What does all this have to do with my dream? My paternal grandfather grew up in Tennessee. At ten years old, he was gone for the weekends. He came back on Monday to take care of his chores. Evidently, his parents didn't care what he did as long as he took care of his responsibilities. When he was twelve or thirteen, my grandfather left home to cut trees in Louisiana. Can you imagine your twelve or thirteen year old working in another state with full grown men? Crazy. He worked hard, and played just as hard.

Until he was fairly old, my grandfather was a rounder. A rounder is a person who frequents and participates in establishments of ill repute. Those activities generally include drinking, fighting, womanizing, and gambling. I knew my grandfather, and he was a good man. I loved him. But, for a long time in his life, he participated in seedy activities. According to family legend, my great-grandfather did too.

My maternal grandfather was an only child raised on a ranch. I've been told he wouldn't even drink coffee, only water. I'm named after him. He also had a reputation for being able to outwork everyone.

Interpretation of dream: From my father's side of the family, I inherited generational curses. These curses found expression in my life through riotous living. I'm not painting a black picture either. Blessings and curses were passed down from both sides of my family. Almost without exception, this is true for everyone. Believe me, every family has skeletons and dirty laundry, as well as good in it. While married for fifteen years, I "let go" of hard living. When I divorced, I took it up again. What's really sad is this: My wife held an idolatrous place in my heart. I stopped partying for her, but not for God. The issue was not riotous living; sin is sin. God exposed my heart as only He can do. I loved someone else more than I loved Him. That's evil.

Shortly after my dream, while I exercised at the gym, the Lord spoke a clear "rhema" word to me. He said that just as Nebuchadnezzar had lost his mind, and lived with the animals for seven years, so had I. [Daniel 4:31-32] As He humbled Nebuchadnezzar, He humbled me. I'm not a national leader or a king, yet because I'm the Lord's favorite son, He disciplined me. A sick mind is an indication of a sick heart. After seven years to the month, the work was finished.

A few of my friends were heroin addicts. A couple of them said, "God healed me just like that. All of a sudden my desire for heroin was gone. No withdrawals—nothin'." I've thought to myself, "Wow, only God could do that." Most folks walk around with a wild monster locked up in their heart. The monster might be heroin, sex, alcohol, greed, jealousy, racism, anger, envy, gossip, unforgiveness or anything else. These beasts are always looking for ways to get out, and do. No one is strong enough to kill them. I'm not, but the Lord is strong enough, and He will. He did it for me, and He will do it for you too. The end of the matter is this,

> *Now I, Nebuchadnezzar [Walter Justice], praise and exalt and glorify the King of heaven, because everything he does is right and all his ways are just. And those who walk in pride he is able to humble.*
> [Daniel 4:37]

INTRODUCTION

You can't stop us on the road to freedom
You can't stop keep us 'cause our eyes can see
VAN MORRISON *TUPELO HONEY*

My heart underwent a transformation. Until now, I never had the freedom to express my journey. I felt like a dog on a leash: I'd start running, and then all of a sudden, I was snapped back off my feet. In other words, I crashed and burned. Eventually, I understood getting "snapped back" was the grace of the Lord. I'm thankful. God does something in us before he does something through us. Daniel 11:35 says,

> *Some of the wise will stumble, so that they may be refined, purified and made spotless until the time of the end, for it will still come at the appointed time.*

Our eyes gravitate to the words "refined, purified, and spotless." If we are really honest with ourselves, we probably think we're wise, or at least a little wiser than the next guy. However, the trigger in this passage is "stumble." We grow when we stumble. Scripture says,

> *Consider it pure joy, my brothers whenever you face trials of many kinds, because you know that the testing of your faith develops*

> *perseverance. Perseverance must finish its work so that you may be mature and complete, not lacking anything.*
> [James 1:2-4]

In my life, perseverance has not finished its work. I'm closer than I've ever been though. The difficulties, the hurts, and even the so-called failures made me who I am.

As I survey the scripture, I cannot find any great man or woman of the faith who did not experience hardship and brokenness. The bible is full of cowards, prostitutes, murderers, and liars who were transformed by the power of God. They became believers of extra-ordinary courage. Fear hides, but courage is transparent. Biblical heroes reveal the glory of God and not personal righteousness. Yet, the biblical standard is rarely found in the church today. Our western culture glories in success. Failure doesn't fit well on resumés and websites. I can honestly say, with perhaps one exception, I never attended a conference where leaders shared real-life battles and struggles from the platform. In fact, the present day norm is to possess a title; apostle so-and-so, prophet so-and-so, or bishop so-and-so.

Hardship and brokenness makes us uncomfortable and even causes pain. God strategically places us in difficult circumstances so that issues of the heart are exposed and hopefully addressed. I've heard countless Christians quote this well known passage,

> *And we know that in all things God works for the good of those who love him, who have been called according to his purpose.*
> [Romans 8:28]

They often flippantly toss out this passage to a brother or a sister in Christ living through difficult and trying times.

However, when our turn comes, which it will and we walk through trying situations, Romans 8:28 takes on a whole new meaning. The phrase "*all things work for the good*" is easier said than believed. Even so, in difficult circumstances, bitterness and disdain need not overtake us. I'm talking about overcoming.

Fire exposes the heart; both godliness and wickedness. Moments of challenge, great crisis and controversy are moments of exposure. We learn who we are. I have the deepest conviction that the Lord orchestrates hot situations. He tells us,

> ... *When you walk through the fire, you will not be burned: the flames will not set you ablaze.* [Isaiah 43:2]

The purpose of fire is to burn away the perishable or dross. Jesus makes it very clear, "*everyone will be salted with fire.*" [Mark 9:49]

If we have the courage to open our hearts and embrace the fire, we will come out on the other side. I'm going to tell you a secret: You will never overcome the world until you overcome yourself. And you will never overcome yourself until you submit to the fire of the Holy Spirit. The Holy Spirit is the Spirit of truth. [John 16:13] The Spirit of truth convicts us of sin. [John 16:9] Most folks confuse guilt and fear with conviction of sin.

Unless a person is a full blown sociopath, they know their wrong doings. Each person possesses an innate sense of right and wrong, or a conscience. Failings create feelings of guilt. When a guilty person hears a condemning sermon, fear is ignited in them. A terrified soul will repeat any formulistic prayer, and do practically anything to stay out of hell. The dilemma remains though; the terrified soul is unchanged. In all likelihood, their situation worsens because they do not have the power in and of themselves to be transformed. A guilty conscience focuses on personal sin.

Conviction of sin is much different. The Holy Spirit makes us aware, or illuminates sin while drawing us to Jesus. I've been in a couple of super hot saunas. Each time, the routine was the same. At first, the heat felt good. However, after a few short minutes, I became aware that my entire body was overheating. I found myself squirming, and staring at the door. I knew relief was on the other side of the door. I got up; walked through the door, and experienced immediate relief. Like a hot sauna, sin feels good at first. Soon though, through the work of the Holy Spirit, we dislike our sin. The Spirit gets us to focus on Jesus. He is seen as the Son of God; the only one who can bring relief and freedom. When we embrace Him, we experience instantaneous relief from sin.

Believing is faith. Relationship determines the degree of faith. For example, I have faith my car will start when I turn the key. I have greater faith in the goodness of my family, even though I can't see them or touch them at this moment. An integral component of faith is commitment. Without commitment, there is no faith. My commitment to my family is worlds apart from my commitment to my car. Faith pursues and acts according to the depth of our commitment. A strong committed relationship is a deep, loving relationship. I completely trust my family, but ultimately my faith rests in God. Faith gives eyes to the heart. When we believe, we see. Jesus says in John 16:33,

> "*...In this world you will have trouble. But take heart! I have overcome the world.*"

God affirms the point made earlier; you and I are going to face difficulties and hardship. Yet, Jesus also encourages. We are told to take heart. Why? Because he, Jesus, the one we believe is the Son of God, overcame the world. What does it mean to overcome? To subdue, to conquer, or overthrow. Jesus literally conquered the world. He is our Lord. If he is our Lord, then we should possess his values and reflect his image. It's easy to determine who or what one worships. Look at their values and image. What a person values and worships, they look like. 1 John 2:6 is clear,

> "*Whomever claims to live in him must walk as Jesus did.*"

We don't modify scripture to fit our personal experience. Rather, we overcome through the power of his Spirit [Ephesians 3:16-19], hindrances that prevented us from walking as Jesus did. He was not dominated by natural appetites, nor seduced by temptations of the enemy. [Matthew 3:2-11] Jesus was not controlled by his earthly family. [Matthew 12:46-50] Finite resources did not prevent Him from blessing others. [Mark 8:1-8] He had enough money. [Matthew 17:24-27] Jesus ruled over sickness and the demonic. [Luke 5:12-13 and Matthew 12:22] The elements submitted to Him. [Mark 4:37-41] He was not manipulated by religious leaders. [John 8:1-11] Even death obeyed Jesus. [John 11:1-44] Since we believe Jesus is the Son of God, then we too, should walk in the same authority and power as He did. In fact, Jesus emphatically assures us we will.

> *I tell you the truth, anyone who has faith in me will do what I have been doing. He will do even greater things than these, because I am going to the Father. And I will do whatever you ask in my name, so that the Son may bring glory to the Father. You may*

ask me for anything in my name, and I will do it. [John 14:12-14]

For many believers, to walk as Jesus did, seems like pie-in-the-sky idealism. Please understand we are in development. We go from glory to glory. [2 Corinthians 3:18] The letters to the seven churches in Revelation 2-4 possess promises to he or she who overcomes. Yet, a more correct, literal rendering reads "*to him who is overcoming.*" [Young, Revelation 2:7] In other words, overcoming is not static, but dynamic and ongoing. Overcoming is process. This book is written for the believer chosen by God to overcome.

I couldn't profile overcomers if I tried. The issue is not gender or race. Socioeconomic status, education, and age are not factors either. Overcomers just won't fit into a nice, neat, little pictures.

Are there common characteristics? Sure. Overcomers possess an insatiable thirst for the deeper things of God. They also experience hardship and difficulties others seem to bypass. While most of us focus on externals, God looks at the heart. [1 Samuel 16:7] And that is the difficulty in identifying these people. Quite simply, overcoming is a spiritual condition, or a heart thing.

Usually every year, Hollywood produces a western film. I'm a big fan of westerns. On opening weekend, I rush to the theater and catch the latest cowboy flick. A lot of westerns have scouts. The role of the scout was to ride ahead of the wagon train or the cattle drive, determine the best route or trail, return, and then guide the others safely through unknown territories.

I consider myself a scout. During my own journey, I have traveled through hostile and dangerous territories. I know where danger lies, as well as the safe places. I've been there. If you'll listen to me, I can guide you to overcoming.

THE ROOT OF THE PROBLEM

Someday I'll fly
Someday I'll soar
Someday I'll be so damn much more
JOHN MAYER *BIGGER THAN MY BODY*

When I was still young, my family moved across town into a new subdivision. Like many new subdivisions, the home owners were required to put in their own yards. My dad took vacation time, and with the help of my grandfather, spent the next week and a few weekends, landscaping. Fig orchards covered the area prior to new homes being built. An old fig stump remained in our backyard. The tree was cut to ground level, yet the stump was still visible. Fresh, young shoots grew out the sides. My dad planted shrubs in front of the stump, plucked the shoots and poured gasoline on it. A short time later, shoots developed again. This time, my dad was killing the stump for sure. He soaked it with the herbicide *RoundUp*. We had to be very careful with this stuff because of the toxicity. The *RoundUp* available then was much more potent than now. Well, that was that. Not! Flash forward several months, and new shoots began to sprout. The stump wouldn't die. Thirty eight years later the stump is now a strong, healthy tree. My father never cut the root. I understand.

Years later I cleaned yards for a family friend. The

owner hired a tree service to cut down an old tree, and haul the wood away. My job was to pluck out the stump. I dug, chopped, hacked, and pried. The stump had huge roots. Eventually, I took a tow chain, tied one end to the mangled stump and the other end to the back of my four-wheel drive truck. After my truck bounced up and down a few times, the stump broke loose. Thick twisted roots clung to the stump.

People are like those trees. Bad behaviors are identified, and cut down. Later on, however, that same behavior, or one like it manifests. Maybe someone struggles with smoking. They know cigarettes are bad for their health. They stop smoking but now drink pots of coffee. Others give up a promiscuous lifestyle and become gym rats. Some folks channel their anger into work.

These remedies are therapeutic gimmicks. Excessive amounts of coffee, exercise, and work are much more acceptable than smoking, promiscuity, or fits of rage. For the culture at large, these gimmicks are reasonable and even ethical. A sculpted body is preferred to a sexually transmitted disease infection.

Contemporary western culture influences Christianity more than Christianity influences contemporary western culture. Most believers readily embrace therapeutic gimmicks. However, if a believer is going to "overcome," those values are unacceptable. Really, sin is simply whitewashed. Believers cover their struggles like everyone else with civility and respectability. The fig tree wouldn't die because the root was never severed. Unless the root is severed in a believer's life, their struggles will continue.

Jesus admonished us to inspect fruit. [Matthew 7:20] Confusion arises over what spiritual fruit is. Jesus continued,

> *Not everyone who says to me, Lord, Lord will enter the kingdom of heaven, but only he who does the will of my Father who is in heaven. Many will say to me on that day, Lord, Lord did we not prophesy in your name and in your name drive out demons and perform many miracles? Then I will tell them plainly, I never knew you. Away from me you evildoers!* [Matthew 7:21-23]

Gifts and works are not fruit. Too often, believers are bewitched. Just because someone moves in revelatory powers does not mean they are in tune with God. Others give away huge sums of money without ever being led by the Spirit. God over abundantly blesses each person with gifts and talents. These faculties function even when a person is not serving the Lord. [Romans 11:29] Conversely,

> *...The fruit of the Spirit is love, joy, peace, patience, kindness, goodness, faithfulness, gentleness, and self-control.*
> [Galatians 5:22-23]

The fruit of the Spirit is the character of God. A person walking in the Spirit exhibits these characteristics. A Godly person's ministry and deeds naturally grow the fruit of the Spirit. If they don't, the source must be questioned, regardless of the supernatural quality or the sacrifice.

Years ago, I managed a carwash. An employee by the name of Red worked for us. He was consistent and hardworking. I wanted to put action to my faith, so I gave Red a car. Soon, Red missed work and wound up in jail. The car was too much temptation for him. Finally, he sold the car and moved to another city. My "sacrifice" was not led by the Spirit, as evidenced by the fruit, and actually led to Red's downfall.

I was also involved in a prophetic ministry. The leader promoted herself as a prophet. She used flattery to woo and hook her victims. I was one of them. Even so, accurate prophetic words flowed. Later on, she told me to avoid a house gathering in another community, because as incredible as it may sound, the local ministerial was setting a trap for me.

I called the minister who supposedly warned her, and asked him about "the trap." He had no idea what I was talking about. She had lied, and I wasn't allowed to attend the gathering. The gathering felt abandoned, and grew angry and bitter. The so-called prophet became increasingly demeaning, especially toward men in local gatherings. In fact, men were scarce.

After one particularly intense gathering, I confronted her with a house leader and two elders. The next day, I was relieved of my responsibilities. Shortly thereafter, she and her overseer told me to leave their ministry, and rescinded my ordination. Many people were hurt and confused. Where was the fruit of the Spirit? There wasn't any. But, the problem was me.

To one degree or another, everyone has experienced deception. For some believers, deception is a recurring theme. As a result, many believers become bitter and cynical. The cycle can be broken though.

To begin with, a person must stop blaming. Finger pointing and accusing isn't going to help anyone. Deception occurs in a person's life because of that person. There is a part of us which agrees with, or participates in the sin being propagated. Maybe we don't manifest or flesh the sin out, or even voice it; nevertheless, the sin resonates with our heart. What do I mean? There is no mixing of light and darkness. Light dispels darkness. As believers, we do not become fixated with evil, or go on witch hunts, but rather, we press into God. What a person beholds, they become. If the focus is on God, they become Godly. If the focus is on education, they become educated.

Like most people, I wanted acceptance. Prophetic ministry possesses a certain mystique and allure. Being recognized as a prophet or possessing a title is more important to some ministers than being Christ-like. The self-proclaimed prophet always keyed on titles. In fact, here is another golden nugget. Where titles are important, beware! Run!

After being given a title and working in the deceptive woman's ministry I felt special. The wickedness of my heart hooked me, and deception ensued. What I am describing is insecurity. Insecurity is pride. What? Yes, insecurity is pride because focus is on self and personal desires.

Insecure people are proud people. When we look to God insecurities fade, and self-reliance disappears. God becomes our source. The leader's boasting, verbal stings and manipulation should have been a red flag for me. Scripture clearly instructs,

> *He chose the lowly things of this world and the despised things – and the things that are not – to nullify the things that are, so that no one may boast before him. It is because of him that you are in Christ Jesus, who has become for us wisdom from God – that is, our righteousness, holiness and redemption. Therefore, as it is written: Let him who boasts boast in the Lord.*
> [1 Corinthians 1:28-31]
>
> *"For out of the overflow of his heart his mouth speaks."* [Luke 6:45]

Proverbs 26:28 says,

> *"A lying tongue hates those it hurts, and a flattering mouth works ruin."*

These verses are straightforward. But, deception by its very nature is blind. My sin, my fault.

Here are two safeguards or strategies for minimizing deception: First of all, know scripture. Few believers really know the word of God. They highlight pet themes and doctrines while ignoring passages which fail to reinforce a present conviction and understanding. Scripture interprets scripture. Passages which seemingly contradict pet themes and doctrines actually balance, and in turn, amplify and enhance understanding. Scripture is the guidepost.

Years ago I worked as a land-leveler. We planted a vineyard. My responsibility was ripping. I drove a Cat D8 tractor, and dragged a multi-ton steel shank. The "ripper," as it was called, tore up hardpan so roots could go deep. If I looked over my shoulder, and watched the shank rip, I swerved and twisted all over the field. The lines were ugly. However, if I looked forward, and focused on a post or telephone pole at the other end of the field, the lines were straight and beautiful. If believers focus on what the word of God says, using it as a guidepost, their lives will be straight.

What about life situations scripture doesn't address? Every day believers are confronted with choices, and a few are significant and important. I've yet to find a scripture which tells me what car to buy, or where to live. Jesus said,

> *"But when he, the Spirit of truth, comes, he will guide you into all truth."* [John 16:13]

If a believer listens, the Spirit of God will speak to them about particulars, and anything else they need to know. The Spirit is the internal Counselor every Christian has. Many believers just don't listen. The voice of the Spirit is kind and gentle. He doesn't push or pull. The Spirit leads.

Believers lose balance too. Either, they ravenously read the word of God and spend little, if any, time praying. Or, they spend hours praying, rarely picking up their bible. The two are not mutually exclusive. The Spirit and the word of God will never contradict each other. The two harmoniously mesh and compliment. If believers want effectiveness, they must learn balance. Balance is not flat-footedness or weighty stability. Balance is maintaining an edge. If a person sharpens one side of a blade, and neglects the other, the blade dulls. Sharpening both sides gets a razor's edge. By studying the word of God and communing with the Father a spiritual edge is maintained.

The second strategy for safeguarding against deception is humility. Anymore, when I meet someone, I watch and listen to their attitude. Who a person is depends upon their attitude of heart or spirit.

Some people are "defeated." Others are demanding. Still others are kind and considerate. Few individuals are able to mask their attitude. Don't get me wrong-- people will try. I've heard statements like, "I only got a seventh grade education," or "I was just born on the wrong side of the tracks." At first, statements like these ring of humility. These phrases sound lowly, don't they? However, each statement is calculated, and is actually saying at a deeper level, "See what I was able to do." Pride always focuses on self.

Humility is also a person's attitude. It is perhaps the truest indicator of godliness. Humility is other-worldly and originates with God. The fruit of the Spirit grows on the tree of humility. A humble person is submissive and teachable. They really do consider others better than themselves. [Philippians 2:3] Humility is real and unpretentious. It cools strife and always seeks the welfare of others.

A couple of years ago, I attended an international conference. During one session, the attendees were instructed to break up into groups of five or six and minister to each other. In my group were four other Americans, myself, and one African. The African looked to be in his late sixties, maybe early seventies. He wore a bright purple suit. I stood next to him, and was a little overwhelmed. The man exuded humility. Every time I closed my eyes, I saw him walking barefoot from village to village, ministering to poor, broken people. The others were hot to get started, and immediately prayed for each other. He stood quietly with his head bowed.
I shared what I saw, and he confirmed my word. Finally, he spoke. His words were soft and simple. Yet, those words carried such force that one young lady wept. We stood in the presence of great humility, and it was unmistakable.

The root of the problem is the human heart. Each person's greatest obstacle continues to be him or herself. Politicians and philanthropists blame disease and poverty for the world's troubles. Christians point the finger at the devil. Everyone wants to blame something or someone. Even so, since the time of Adam and Eve, the wickedness of each heart has contributed to the darkness in the world. If we stomp out AIDs or even hunger, something else just as deadly will rise up.

Remember the story of the fig tree. The tree would not die because the roots were never severed. The evil in our lives will not die until we deal with the wickedness of our own heart.

In John 14, Jesus speaks to his disciples. He tells the twelve about the future. At the end of the chapter, in

John 14:30, Jesus makes a simple yet extremely profound statement.

> *I will not speak with you much longer, for the prince of this world is coming. He has no hold on me...*

I use the New International Version of the bible. However, like most translations, the NIV occasionally fails to capture the essence and depth of a particular passage. A literal, English rendering is "*In me he hath nothing...*" [Young, John 14:30] The critical piece here is *in* instead of *on*. So, why is *in me* so important? Jesus said,

> *For out of the heart come evil thoughts, murder, adultery, sexual immorality, theft, false testimony, slander.* [Matthew 15:19]

Mark 7:21-23 expresses the truth slightly differently,

> *For from within, out of men's hearts, come evil thoughts, sexual immorality, theft, murder, adultery, greed, malice, deceit, lewdness, envy, slander, arrogance, and folly. All these evils come from inside and make a man unclean.*

He also said,

> "*For where your treasure is, there your heart will be also.*" [Luke 12:34]

The heart of Jesus was absolutely surrendered to the Father. Satan could find "no hooks" in Him. There was nothing to bite into since Jesus could not be seduced, pushed, pulled, manipulated, coaxed, intimidated, or deceived by Satan. Jesus came in the flesh, but He was as transparent as a ghost. He had the purest heart ever. This is why He told us,

> *...Love the Lord your God with all your heart with all your soul and with all your mind. This is the first and greatest commandment.* [Matthew 22:37-38]

The heart or Spirit is the core of one's being. From the heart flow the issues of life. Joshua and Caleb were the only two of an entire generation that left Egypt to enter the Promise Land. Even Moses didn't enter. Scripture says Caleb got to go in "b*ecause he followed the Lord whole-heartedly.*" [Deuteronomy 16:36] Not only was Caleb allowed to enter, but he took the choicest of land, and drove out giants living in the region. [Joshua 15:13-17]

The problem is us. Few believers have given their entire heart to the Lord. They want salvation, but not at the cost of surrender and death. The cross always precedes the crown. Many believers want cheap, inexpensive resurrection power.

When John the Baptist prepared the way of the Lord, everyone, including Jesus, needed baptism. No one was exempt. Jesus was without sin, nevertheless, his life, like everyone else, had to be completely and totally surrendered to the Father. Jesus the carpenter ended, and Jesus the Christ began. Water baptism is an action demonstrating complete surrender and death to self, and life and commitment to God. Often, however, water baptism is nothing more than a formality, or a hoop to jump through for many believers. This is why John rebuked the Pharisees and the Sadducees. [Matthew 3:7-8] They pursued form or image, but lacked wholehearted sincerity. When one sincerely repents, and is baptized, the relationship begins. A believer is not transformed overnight. However, if a believer walks out the relationship, they will overcome. We change, God doesn't. He's perfect, we're not. Jesus said,

> *Anyone who loves his father or mother more than me is not worthy of me; anyone who loves his son or daughter more than me is not worthy me; anyone who does not take up his cross and follow me is not worthy of me. Whoever finds his life will lose it, and whoever loses his life for my sake will find it.* [Matthew 12:37-39]

The cross hurts yet, a believer can enter a secret place where they glory in suffering. Eventually, they come to understand that taking up their cross is an honor and privilege. The Lord becomes supreme in the life of a believer.

Satan is able to "hook" believers because of the wickedness of their heart. In other words, he has something in them. I know. I can hear some folks screaming, "I'm a blood bought, born again believer! He has no authority over me!" Really? Then why aren't you more victorious? Why the habitual sins? Why aren't you doing the greater miracles? I'm not throwing stones at anyone, and I can say with Paul that I am the worst of sinners. [1Timothy 1:15] To be real, as I've picked up my cross, I've kicked, screamed, and cried. I'm dying hard.

Most of us like sin. Sin feels good. A believer may not punch someone in the face, but they beat them down in their heart. They may not flirt with a coworker, but they look at her and lust. Jesus said,

> *But I tell you that anyone who looks at a woman lustfully has already committed adultery with her*

> *in his heart.* [Matthew 5:28]

Presently, a theology is circulating which insists our defeatist Christian living stems from wrong thinking. The Alcoholics Anonymous [AA] people call this "stinkin' thinkin'." Their doctrine has biblical foundations:

> *Do not conform any longer to the pattern of this world, but be transformed by the renewing of your mind.* [Romans 12:2]

Without renewing the mind, overcoming is not possible. All of us have developed stinkin' thinkin', or ungodly belief systems.

In fact, even the fiber of our flesh has sinful memory. In body building and weight training experts refer to "muscle memory." This means muscle easily "remembers" the rigors and the expansion it has experienced. So, if a person stops training, even for a significant amount of time, and then begins again, the muscle, because of its memory, quickly responds. Flesh quickly remembers and responds to sin. One can feel the "rush" come over them. Overcoming requires the entire being; heart, soul, and body. [1 Thessalonians 5:23]

The weakness of the wrong thinking doctrine is that it hacks at branches and fruit, but not the roots. Thinking originates from the motives and intentions of the heart. Adam and Eve were pure and sinless with undefiled thinking. Yet, because of the desires of their heart, they were drawn into sin. It's a heart issue. If you get the heart, you get the head. But, just because you get the head, does not mean you get the heart. Also, the wrong thinking doctrine can easily slide into ancient Gnosticism. That is, if believers reach a higher state of consciousness or enlightenment, they will cure earthly limitations and woes. Positive thinking and Christian Science are nothing more than modern versions of Gnosticism.

Believers are watched. Demonic entities know what they do in public and private. Even in the womb, believers were targeted. As a result, satanic forces exploit wounds, as well as genuine godly wants and desires. Satan salts wounds so believers turn to anything except God. He attempts to pervert godliness too. What do I mean? By being created in the very image of God [Genesis 1:27], people possess certain innate characteristics or traits which will always be with them. It's their nature. In other words, God-likeness cannot be repented of, or discarded. In the Garden of Eden, Satan manipulated Eve's innate desire for God-likeness by coaxing her into eating from the forbidden Tree of Knowledge of Good and Evil. [Genesis 3:1-6] Adam, even living in a perfect state, possessed a God-given need for a suitable helper. [Genesis 2:18] He knowingly ate the forbidden fruit with Eve, thereby placing relational primacy with his helper above and beyond his Creator. Since Adam and Eve ate from the Tree of Knowledge of Good and Evil, humankind continues to engage life through good and evil or right and wrong. That is, "what's good for me, and what's bad for me." The grid of good and evil is wholly self-centered. Without the Lord, people attempt to satisfy their innate God-given desires via the Tree of Knowledge of Good and Evil.

Everyone possesses a desire for power. Even in the church, the vast majority of people address this need by manipulating and intimidating others according to their will. Without special grace from God, people naturally yearn for companionship. Once again, however, they become perverse. Especially for men, the global sexual explosion is nothing more than a weak, shallow effort at satisfying their desire for intimacy and companionship. In his book *There Were Two Trees In The Garden*, Rick

Joyner refers to the Tree of Knowledge of Good and Evil as the tree of law. [Joyner 10] 1 Corinthians 15:56 reads, "*...and the power of sin is the law.*"

Once again, James 1:15 says,

> "*...sin, when it is full grown, gives birth to death.*"

So, death comes from sin, and sin is powered by law, and the law starts with the Tree of Knowledge of Good and Evil.

The more rules and regulations there are, the less God. Consider prisons. Prisons are the most regulated institutions on the face of the earth: when to rise, eat, shower, who one can associate with, areas on and off limits, what one can and can't have, where to sleep, who visits, etc. Most believers agree prisons are godless institutions. Other institutions that emphasize "do's and don'ts" are traditional churches. You figure that one out.

The Tree of Life was found in the Garden of Eden too. [Genesis 2:9] Adam and Eve were allowed to eat from this tree. [Genesis 2:16] Obviously, the Tree of Life produces life-giving fruit. The Tree of Knowledge of Good and Evil produces fruit in keeping with good and evil. The former, the Tree of Life, brings about eternal life [Genesis 3:22], and the latter brings about death. [Genesis 2:17]

Jesus is the Tree of Life. When a person partakes of Jesus they enter into eternal life. John 1:4 says, "*In him was life, and that life was the light of men.*"

Jesus said of Himself,

> *I am the way and the truth and the life. No one comes to the Father except through me.* [John 14:6]

And Matthew 26:26-28 says,

While they were eating, Jesus took bread, gave thanks and broke it, and gave it to his disciples, saying, 'Take and eat; this is my body.' Then he took the cup, gave thanks and offered it to them, saying, Drink from it, all of you. This is my blood of the covenant, which is poured out for many for the forgiveness of sins.

Jesus allows believers to reenter Garden life or pre-Fall existence with the Father. I am convinced that if Adam and Eve would have eaten from the Tree of Life (Jesus) first, eventually the Lord would have allowed them to eat from the Tree of Knowledge of Good and Evil. Life with God always centers on foundation and primacy. The Kingdom of God stands on the chief cornerstone, Jesus. [Ephesians 2:20] Believers are called to wield earth shaking power, as long as God takes primacy.

It isn't contrary to the Kingdom of God to have a beautiful spouse, once again, as long as God takes primacy. Believers must be rooted, founded, grounded, tied into, established, living for, seeking, and partaking of the author and finisher of their faith, the Lord Jesus Christ. [Hebrews 12:2]

Here is a practical tip. A person who is partaking of Jesus is rarely concerned with right and wrong. They focus on life, and what fosters life in others. These believers allow themselves to be wronged if being wronged helps someone else. [1 Corinthians 6:7] Conversely, those who continue to eat from the Tree of Knowledge of Good and Evil are overly concerned with right and wrong. They need to be right because right translates into good for them. These people send emails after a heated discussion to have the "last" word. Or, they call others garnishing support for themselves. The secret is not identifying others who act like this, but rather, asking one's self, "Do I?"

Friedrich Nietzsche said if we knew "why," then we could live through "how." [Nietzsche 417] Once again, believers struggle because Satan hooks their heart. Our own wickedness snares and torments us. There is a way out though. The overcoming is painful, but well worth the journey.

CLEANING HOUSE

I have seen peace, I have seen pain
Resting on the shoulders of your name
Do you see the truth through all their lies?
Do you see the world through troubled eyes?
And if you want to talk about it anymore,
Lie here on the floor and cry on my shoulder,
I'm a friend.
JAMES BLUNT *CRY*

There are six pitfalls which consistently prevent people from getting a new heart, or a heart of flesh: rejection, unforgiveness, victimization, self-righteousness, sin consciousness, and idolatry. The prophet Ezekiel prophesied,

> *I will give them an undivided heart and put a new spirit in them; I will remove from them their heart of stone and give them a heart of flesh. Then they will follow my decrees and be careful to keep my laws. They will be my people, and I will be their God.* [Ezekiel 11:19-20]

The prophet is saying God's people shall have a heart of flesh, or a tender heart, rather than a heart of stone, or a hard heart. Believers regularly verbally bite or chastise someone else. Believers make worldly valuations, and excuse poor behavior as strength. I can't count the times I've heard statements like, "Oh she's just strong," or "He's just opinionated." What the world calls strong is weak in the kingdom of God, and what the world views as weak, is really strong. The closer a person draws to God, the more they become like Him. He is not an ageless tyrant, but a tender hearted Father desiring the best for all His creation. How do I know? Once again, scripture says, those who have seen Jesus have seen the Father. [John 14:9] Jesus loved and cared for all. He even forgave those who crucified Him. [Luke 23:34]

The first pitfall is rejection. It has the dreadful power of reinforcing the other five pitfalls. Believers and nonbelievers alike encounter rejection. Nothing is uglier or more painful than getting kicked to the curb. Betrayal, the most spiteful form of rejection, kills a person's spirit. I'd rather get a physical beating. When someone throws another person away, they are essentially saying, "you're not worth the effort" or "I'm better off without you." Rejection is the antithesis of love. It chisels away at the image of God found in each person. I'm not referring to getting turned down for a date, or cut from a sports team; often, a person is not meant to be with someone or do certain things. That's life. Rather, I'm referring to close and meaningful relationships. Friends are supposed to have your back. When they reject you, there's nothing worse. Thank God for Jesus though. Scripture says,

> *For we do not have a high priest who is unable to sympathize with our weaknesses, but we have one who has been tempted in every way, just as we are – yet without sin.*
> [Hebrews 4:15]

Jesus can, and does see the believer through

anything, even betrayal. Don't forget, virtually everyone rejected Jesus. Many believers highlight Peter's three denials. [John 18:15-27] Yet, all the disciples ran out on Him. He understands rejection better than anyone else. Jesus walked me through my hurt, and He'll do the same for you.

Shortly after I married my first wife, she was diagnosed with the incurable disease lupus. I knew God healed. We sought any and all ministries who prayed for the sick. Nothing changed. Eventually, I heard about the gracious, little old lady I spoke of in the Prologue. She prayed for hard cases, and ministered to us. The disease was demonically rooted, and my ex-wife was instantaneously healed. The next day, she did things she wasn't able to do for years.

Friends and family came to meetings. We witnessed miracles, but one friend really struggled. Each time he read his bible or attended church, he fell asleep. He couldn't stay awake. As a child, he was sexually molested. A demon entered his life via the abuse. He came to a meeting, and we cast a spirit of molestation out of him. The bizarre sleepiness left with the demon.

Later, my friend, his wife and my ex-wife decided I was too involved with deliverance ministry. They believed the little old lady was controlling. She had those issues. The three recruited a prophet type to confront me. I was sat down in a room, with a couple of complete strangers, and put in the middle of a circle. They told me the little old lady was evil, and I was deceived. My wife just sat there, and never said one word on my behalf. I was crushed. Afterwards, every time I heard my inquisitor's name, I went ballistic. It took me a long time to forgive him and the others, especially my ex-wife. But, that was only the beginning.

My ex-wife was a school teacher. All of a sudden,

she stopped talking about work. Something was wrong. One day, while in prayer, Lord told me she was having an affair. My heart sank. I needed to say something.
I shared what the Lord spoke to me, and she cried. My ex-wife said she was emotionally involved with another teacher, but she hadn't slept with him. She promised the affair was over. I laid in bed and cried. I knew I had to forgive, so I did.

Sometimes people think they don't have to forgive, especially if they deem another's sin as atrocious or heinous. I simply remind myself of the forgiveness extended to me by God. Remember, our ultimate standard is not each other, but the Lord. If someone feels like they have the right to throw stones, be my guest.

My next rejection was public. We attended seminary. One professor decided to really push the envelope. He invited a transvestite to come and lecture our class on alternative lifestyles. He also took a class to visit local Native Americans. The Native Americans decided the students needed "cleansing." They lit a concoction, and blew smoke on the students. Then, the professor insinuated creation was an erotic experience for God. This latest provocation pushed me over the edge. I discussed my concerns with him and the dean of students. Frustration and anger grew.

An open meeting was scheduled for anyone with a grievance. A colleague, as well as a couple students came in support of the professor in question. The dean of students presided. Of all the concerned students, only two of us made an appearance. My ex-wife avoided the meeting. Three PhDs and two students chewed me up and spit me out. Supposedly, people are confined to "anthropomorphic" [human attributes] language in depicting God and His ways. In a certain respect, this is true. However, the attitude behind the professor's comments and instruction was not humility searching for understanding, but one of smugness and provocation. A few students and professors branded me as a fundamentalist on the lunatic fringe. I was hurt. It hurt more when my wife wouldn't stand with me.

When we lived in Canada, my home front crumbled. My ex-wife fell into deep depression and hid in our house. She couldn't conceive, and so we went through a battery of infertility tests, as well as surgery and invitro fertilization. We never got pregnant. Gradually, she wouldn't venture out of the house if small children were present. A couple of times, guests stayed with us, and she never left our bedroom except to eat or use the bathroom. Our guests never met her, let alone saw her.

I became desperate. I confessed any sin that came to mind. I fasted until my body broke down. Life got worse. I unraveled. During our marriage, I never shared any hurts or disappointments about my ex-wife with anyone. I took the view my responsibility was to protect her, and I did. However, the feelings weren't mutual.

People became concerned. They believed I was increasingly unstable. I went on antidepressants. Someone suggested I consider shock treatment.

Although I was quite a bit younger than my clergy peers, nevertheless, I took the lead. Even though I constantly interacted and ministered to a wide variety of people, I was isolated and alone. Years later, my family said to me, "You never told us anything about the situation between you and __ (my ex-wife)."

Eventually, my ex-wife pursued adoption. Life got uglier. Two adoptions fell through, one a week before the baby was due. We had deaths in our families. I wept all the time. I'd walk into a grocery store, and cry. Also, my gall bladder was removed. I continued eating pain medication for kidney stones. I became a pill junkie.

A couple in our church whose young daughter was

still in high school became pregnant. She wanted us to adopt her baby. We got the little guy right out of the hospital! However, under Canadian law, adoptions aren't finalized until after six months. During that season, my ex-wife treated me like I was the greatest man in the world. Yet, on the phone, she told everyone else, including my family, I was a horrible man.

My slide continued. Eventually, I had difficulty walking up the stairs in our house. After an extended fast, I went from 200 pounds down to 150 pounds on my six-foot tall frame. People thought I'd come from a death camp. Spiritually, I was tapped out too. I lost my passion for the Lord, and especially for people. Life was dark.

We took a well-needed three month sabbatical. My family and others encouraged us to come home. A big surprise awaited me. When we arrived in California, my family berated me and I couldn't understand why. Once again, my wife sat there and just listened. Over the last few months, she had assassinated me over the phone. I cracked. All I could think about was running. Who can you trust if not your wife and family? I rented a car, and left for Las Vegas.

In Sin City, I drank, smoked, and went to a strip club. Pain and paranoia gripped me. Even in my dark hole, God was in control and began bringing me to the end of myself. God exposed Walter. Regardless of my treatment and pain, my behavior was unjustifiable. After one day in Las Vegas, I drove home. During the six hour journey, an overwhelming compulsion to swerve into oncoming traffic seized me. By God's grace, I arrived home safely. I told my ex-wife what I did in Las Vegas.

We entered counseling. I was prescribed an extremely high dosage of antidepressants. After another month, my family saw the other side of my ex-wife. Counseling wasn't particularly helpful either; a PhD doesn't make one insightful.

My ex-wife felt I needed tell someone else about the Las Vegas trip. I stopped caring. My overseer was in town, and so I confessed to him. I also informed my wife I would tell anyone else she wanted me to, including our little church. According to her, my slate was clean. My father warned me not to go back to Canada-- he was right.

When we arrived in Canada, I met with church leadership. I asked if they wanted to hear about my sabbatical, "No, not really." They told me about the financial situation of the church along with other important stuff. I signed a medical release form with my family physician which allowed the church leadership to discuss my wellbeing with him.

After a couple of months, the antidepressants worked overtime. I went through the ceiling. Superman had nothing on me. People noticed a change in me, and even my personality was altered.

After church one Sunday, a group which included my ex-wife, sat me down in a back room. (Sound familiar?) My wife had told her girlfriends about Las Vegas, and in turn those busybodies informed the church leadership. My accusers called me a hypocrite and a liar. "How dare you waste the church's money in Las Vegas!" Two members of church leadership said I lied to them. Supposedly, they had inquired about my time off. Once again, my wife sat with the others, and just stared at me. I slammed my fist, cussed, and walked out. I was done.

My chest killed me; I couldn't stop the pain. I went to see my family physician, but I forgot how to get there; I had lived in the community for five years. I ate all my pain killers, but found no relief. My parents called, and were horrified. They feared something worse might happen, maybe even death. I just shut down. In Canada, pharmacies sell Tylenol with codeine over the counter. After my pain medication ran out, I ate Tylenol with codeine. My ex-wife had prescription medication too. I took thirty-four migraine pills in a couple of hours. Nothing helped. My ex-wife considered institutionalizing me.

A couple of days later, my father booked a flight for me, and I went home. When I arrived in California, I really freaked out--my pills were gone. I lost everything except the clothes on my back. I jumped in my parent's car and took off. I was desperate. I found some crack, and smoked it.

When people are desperate, they're capable of anything. A person may say to themselves, "No, not me." Trust me; if a person hurts badly enough, they'll do whatever it takes to stop the pain. I hadn't bottomed out though, and professionals kept me on a high dosage of antidepressants.

With my family's help, I bought a motorcycle. For the next five years, I rode bikes. My medication made me feel indestructible too. One afternoon, I saw a pretty young woman standing on a street corner. I asked her if she wanted a ride, but she wanted a "date." She kept pestering me, and I finally agreed. The woman was an undercover officer, and so the police detained me.

On the street, the term "date" means sex. I couldn't believe what happened to me. However, through this drama, I met a psychologist. I told her I felt like dying. One minute, I was Superman, and in the next, I crashed and looked for a rock to crawl underneath. Although I couldn't pay her, she still helped me. (Throughout my life, wherever I've gone, I've met good people; they're everywhere, even in the most unlikely places.) The psychologist ran tests, including ink blots, and determined my medication needed modification. In hindsight, I think God used her to save my life. I was diagnosed as Bipolar.

Over the next couple of years my eyes opened to a

different world. A humbling began in my heart. I learned I was no better than anyone else. I believe Margaret Thatcher alluded to the fact that a very thin veneer of civility covers society. My veneer was ripped off!

I began working with juvenile delinquents. My new friends were former outlaws and gangsters. Order began to return to my life. I quit my medication cold turkey. I wouldn't recommend this to anyone. For about a week or week and a half, every time I took a step, my head felt as though it was a couple of feet behind me. Like most medications, a gradual weaning of antidepressants is the best way.

For about four or five months, I completely stopped smoking and drinking. I didn't hang out at biker bars anymore. However, my dark days weren't over yet.

A mutual friend introduced me to my second wife. She was beautiful, and from the get-go, I was mesmerized. My first wife had come from a wealthy background, was college educated, a teetotaler, and very respectable. I wasn't going there again. If she was white, I wanted black. If she went right, I turned left. No more fake for me. My second wife seemed like just the opposite of my first wife, or so I thought. She liked motorcycles, wore leather, smoked and drank beer, played pool, and grew up on the poorer side of town. Perfect. Wrong!

I was still so broken that one of the first times I tried to share my heart with her, I smoked a pack of cigarettes in about forty minutes. I took up my old vices again. We hung out with her friends, most of whom liked to party. After a few months, we were married.

She pressured me into distancing myself from my friends, and I did. She didn't like where I worked either, so I quit. From her perspective, I had serious issues since I'd been married and divorced. Ironically, her mother had been married five or six times, and she had been married three times prior to me. According to her, I was too up and down.

Determined to make my new marriage last, I sought out a Christian counselor. I found a Christian psychologist who counseled and prayed with me. The experience was helpful and therapeutic. The psychologist encouraged me to restart my medication. Yet, he soon realized a major part of my problem was my wife.

Before being married to me, she underwent three years of counseling. She believed her life was altogether. However, there is a distinction between coping, and being truly healed. My counselor also believed a strong demonic entity worked in her life. Remember, sometimes people like their stuff. Within ten months, she divorced me.

One of the last times I saw her, God opened my eyes. We sat on our back porch, and as I looked at her face, it flickered: her face, then an old woman's; her face, then an old woman's. This went on for a couple of minutes. I was dealing with a Jezebel spirit. My sister has a dear friend who is a psychiatrist. She had met both wives. She felt I married a woman just like my first wife; extremely narcissistic. A different wrapper doesn't necessarily mean a different package. I was left with nothing except about a $17,000 debt.

The second pitfall, unforgiveness, is reinforced by the first, rejection. If a person lives long enough, they will be wronged, and some of them will be severely wronged. Scripture refers to wrongs as offence. People hurt and wound each other. We are told,

> *Get rid of all bitterness, rage and anger, brawling and slander, along with every form of malice. Be kind and compassionate to one another, forgiving each other, just as in Christ God forgave you.* [Ephesians 4:31-32]

A believer can seek forgiveness from others. Sometimes the offended forgive, and sometimes they don't forgive. Nevertheless, the believer's part is seeking forgiveness. My experience has taught me that if a person approaches others with a contrite, humble heart, the offended are much more willing to extend forgiveness and commence restoration. This is a God standard. God, in His infinite love, forgave us our sins by providing His son Jesus as an atoning sacrifice. 1 John 1:7-10 says,

> *...And the blood of Jesus, his Son, purifies us from all sin. If we claim to be without sin, we deceive ourselves and the truth is not in us. If we confess our sins, he is faithful and just and will forgive us our sins and purify us from all unrighteousness. If we claim we have not sinned, we make him out to be a liar and his word has no place in our lives.*

Forgiveness is love. God loves us, so He forgives us when we embrace His son Jesus. In turn, believers are able to love because He first loved us. [1 John 4:19] The greatest commandment is love God, and the second is like it, love your neighbor. [Matthew 22:37-40] It also says in 1 John 4:20-21,

> *If anyone says, I love God, yet hates his brother, he is a liar. For anyone who does not love his brother, whom he has seen, cannot love God, whom he has not seen. And he has given us this command:*
>
> *Whoever loves God must also love his brother.*

I have encountered a lot of hate in the body of Christ. Hate translates into unforgiveness. I've listened to long elaborate prayers, seen tears, witnessed handshakes, and yet, unforgiveness resides in many, many hearts. Jesus said we have to forgive from our heart. [Matthew 18:35] Many Christians forgive in their minds, but not their hearts.

How do I know? Here are a couple of simple, practical tests. When a person hears a name, or discusses a past event, do their emotions flare? Anger? Rage? Grief? Do they feel the need to tell others how bad or evil a person or ministry is? If these questions ring true, in all likelihood, a person has unforgiveness. They can attend all the self help groups and therapy in the world, and still find no relief. Drugs, sex, and rock-n-roll provide only momentary relief. Prescription drugs are more controlled, yet, serve the same numbing function as illegal narcotics.

Even bizarre, elusive diseases like lupus, fibromyalgia, and arthritis are rooted in unforgiveness. I knew a woman who snarled every time the conversation moved to her deceased father. She was sexually abused by him, and suffers from fibromyalgia. Women seemingly possess a greater ability to disengage the mind from the heart than do men. I'm not saying every physical ailment has a spiritual source. The view "all disease" is spiritually entrenched is naïve and simplistic, and even unbiblical. [John 9:1-3] Both men and women tuck unforgiveness into the basements of their hearts, but eventually, one way or another, unforgiveness manifests or crawls out.

A pastor, who was instrumental in the salvation of my father, was ousted by a church. To the day he died, he refused to forgive. He died from a very aggressive cancer. Many of us have lived through horrific ordeals and circumstances. By no means do I want to trivialize someone's pain. I'm not. Nevertheless, unless a person forgives from the heart, they will be tormented in this life, and the life to come. God is very clear,

> *For if you forgive men when they sin against you, your Heavenly Father will also forgive you. But if you do not forgive men their sins, your Father will not forgive your sins.* [Matthew 6:14-15]

A third and extremely insidious stronghold is victimization. Victimization is insidious because a person rarely takes ownership or responsibility for their actions, or lack thereof. Have you ever met a person who is stuck in the past? Who rarely, if ever, can say "I was wrong," or even, "Thank you." Once a person walks towards the future, or takes ownership for their actions, or demonstrates gratitude, they are no longer a victim. A person stuck in the past is saying, "See what happened to poor me." It is a manipulative ploy for gaining sympathy. To say, "I was wrong" implies offense, and once a person is an offender, they can no longer be a victim. To show gratitude or appreciation demonstrates they were the recipient of charity, and that no one owed them a thing.

The welfare mentality, as it is resentfully known, is nothing more than mass victimization. Victims play the blame game. If blame is placed on another, then they're not responsible. They cling to past wrongs, which is unforgiveness, in order to excuse their own sinfulness. Proverbs 10:12 says,

> *"Hatred stirs up dissention, but love covers over all wrongs."*

A close friend was severely abused as a child, and I

mean severely. He became a gangster, worked for a gang, and was in and out of prison throughout his life. During his last incarceration, he was saved. Upon release, a number of ministries asked him to share his testimony. Over time, I discerned a pattern. His testimony always focused on his mistreatment, and rarely, if ever, on what he had done wrong. He was extremely narcissistic. My friend always drew attention to himself, and his ministry.

Victimization is fueled by unforgiveness. Victims don't forget. Some professionals say a person is not supposed to forget, nor can they forget. I strongly disagree. When a person really forgives, the wrong is forgotten. Can a person recall an offense if they really want to? Sure. But that's the point; it takes effort and focus to remember the wrong. Scripture says,

> *Love is patient, love is kind. It does not envy, it does not boast, it is not proud. It is not rude, it is not self-seeking, it is not easily angered, it keeps no record of wrongs.* [1 Corinthians 13:4-6]

Victims are low-level survivors. What do I mean? Victims, often because of mistreatment, learn to depend on themselves to survive. With survival, a person does anything to stay afloat. By its very nature, survival excludes security and peace. Victims have rarely lived in secure, peaceful environments. Fear creeps in, and self-serving survival techniques take over. Since a person is shoved into chaotic circumstances, their view is; "It's not my fault," or "I've been wronged," or ‘I'm the victim."

Higher-level survivors are found in Alcoholics Anonymous (AA) and Narcotics Anonymous (NA). These folks momentarily stop their self-destructive cycles. The 12-step programs force participants to acknowledge their own wrongdoing, and actually seek forgiveness and restitution. Nevertheless, these programs fail to raise a person above survivor status. The program reinforces once an addict, always an addict. Twelve-step programs help participants recognize something greater than themselves, namely a higher power. Many recovering addicts are Christians, yet, Jesus Christ is still unable to completely heal them of their addictions. The twelve-stepper develops healthy structures, accountability, and the ability to say "no." Programming cages the monsters inside them. There is a foreboding fear that if the monster or the addiction is ever freed, once again, it will ravage their life. For the recovering addict, the monster is too powerful to kill. It is. Only the power of God can kill an addiction. The bible says,

> "*With man this is impossible, but with God all things are possible.*" [Matthew 19:26]

Often, a person unknowingly fortifies sin in others. I have a gift of mercy, and so, I'm merciful. But, there is such a thing as unsanctified mercy. That is, sometimes God's best for someone is not mercy. Mercy becomes perverted when not Spirit led.

In my two previous marriages, both women were victims. I had codependent relationships with them. Codependency is a psychological buzz word these days, and few people fully understand the implications. From a Christian perspective, codependency contributes to another's sinfulness. Instead of peanut butter and jelly, or complimenting each other, it is gasoline and fire, and the fire burns until everything is gone. I would coddle "woe is me" or "life's unfair" attitudes. In so doing, my mercy gift was used in a sick, ungodly manner.

Giftings function even when were not serving the Lord. Many great salesmen are meant to evangelize. Some psychics are ungodly prophets. A few power-hungry CEOs are unsanctified apostles. Either one's giftings will serve the Lord, and establish His Kingdom, or they serve themselves, and enhance darkness. For this reason, a person must understand who they are, and the motives of their heart.

In Matthew 25:14-30, there is the famous parable of the talents. Most readers highlight the reaping; the good servants used what was given, and received more [vs 19-23], while the wicked servant hid his talents, and lost them. [vs 24-30] However, the overarching theme or significance of the parable deals with motivation. The good servants were exactly that, serving the interest of their master. The wicked servant was concerned for his personal welfare; he was more afraid of failing than blessing his master. Many believers are serving themselves, and not the Lord. This is why believers are admonished,

> *...seek first his kingdom and his righteousness, and all these things will be given to you as well.* [Matthew 6:33]

The fourth hindrance or heart issue is self-righteousness. Some believers, especially the woo-woo types, call this the pharisaical spirit. It is. Often, Christians use demonic activity to excuse poor behavior. I remember watching the Flip Wilson Show. [Wilson] He came out dressed in drag as Geraldine. Geraldine's standard excuse was, "The devil made me do it!" I've come to believe that there are a lot of "Geraldine's" in Christendom, even among the leaders. Yes, there are demonic entities completely committed to the believer's downfall and ruin. Where there is poop, there are flies (demonic). Where there is trash, there are rats (demonic). If a Christian wants to get rid of flies and rats, start by getting rid of personal sin. There is a demonic entity which could be characterized as a pharisaical spirit, or at least, a religious spirit. Believers have to ask themselves why these spirits are afflicting them. Generally, demonic spirits are able to torment believers because of the condition of their hearts.

Soren Kierkegaard was a nineteenth century philosopher. Scholarship credits Kierkegaard as being the father of modern day existentialism. From a Christian perspective, he was a prophet who challenged the hypocrisy and the excesses of the Danish church. He cited three stages in human life. [Storm]

First, there is the aesthetic. People live according to the sensory; vivid colors, attraction and repulsion, smells and all the like. Secondly, if one progresses, they enter the ethical. These people realize laws and civility are beneficial, and require commitment and decision. Life is more than "eat, drink and be merry." The third stage is spirituality or the internal life lived in relation to God.

The great scientific thinker Michael Polanyi expressed a similar understanding. He identified three levels too. [Polanyi 394-405] The most basic level is the phenomenal or sensory; see, taste, smell, touch, and hearing. Then, there is the functional. Particulars are identified and worked or utilized. The third level is the semantic. Meaning comes from integrating these particulars.

1 Thessalonians 5:23 says,

> *...May your whole spirit, soul, and body be kept blameless at the coming of our Lord Jesus Christ.*

People are physical, and therefore they sense and physically interact with their surroundings. We have a soul, and process information. Finally, people have a spirit where meaning and significance, or our deepest understanding and awareness resides.

There is the well used passage in which Jesus dialogued with the religious leader Nicodemus. [John 3:1-21] Jesus told Nicodemus he must be born again. At this, Nicodemus was completely baffled. [vs 3-4] He functioned on the second level. As a religious leader, he was moral and ethical. Nicodemus studied law and knew information, obviously applying it to his own life, and as a leader, to the lives of others. He was a soulish man though. Nicodemus was dead to the third level; the internal life with God; the place of meaning and significance; or, spiritual life. [vs 6-8]

Let me biblically spin this train of thought:

> *Then the voice that I heard from heaven spoke to me once more: Go take the scroll that lies open in the hand of the angel who is standing on the sea and on the land. So I went to the angel and asked him to give me the little scroll. He said to me, Take it and eat it. It will turn your stomach sour, but in your mouth it will be sweet as honey. I took the little scroll from the angel's hand and ate it. It tasted as sweet as honey in my mouth, but when I had eaten it, my stomach turned sour. Then I was told, You must prophesy again about many peoples, nations, languages, and kings.*
> [Revelation 10:8-11]

First of all, the apostle John, the writer of Revelation, knew the scroll was from God. Most people, including unbelievers, can discern basic truth. People from all walks of life agree with the famous adage, "*do to others what you would have them do to you.*" [Matthew 7:12]

This is the most basic level of truth; the validity is easily recognizable.

Next, John ate the scroll and it tasted as sweet as honey. Believers, and unbelievers alike, begin to recognize biblical principles, and apply them to their life. Psalm 34:8 says, "*Taste and see that the Lord is good.*" These principles or standards are sweet because they work.

Mormons tapped into the wisdom literature of scripture, and they prosper. The Faith Movement is predicated upon knowing and understanding principles of faith. Since faith is an intrinsic characteristic of God, it is woven into the very fabric of life. Believers who move in this stream understand faith is like a natural principle; when harnessed properly, faith greatly blesses.

Thirdly, John's stomach turned sour. This is the deepest level of truth. Believers digest the word of God, and it literally becomes a part of them. They actually live the word. Their lives are walking, breathing messages. However, herein lies the rub. 1 John 2:15-16 says,

> *Do not love the world or anything in the world. If anyone loves the world, the love of the Father is not in him. For everything in the world – the cravings of the sinful man, the lust of his eyes and the boasting of what he has and does – comes not from the Father but from the world.*

A believer's life is no longer lived in this realm, but in the age to come. The Truth is in them [John 15:4-8], and as they engage the world, their presence exposes sin. This is why scripture says,

> "*Do not be surprised, my brothers, if the world hates you.*" [1 John 3:13]

There is an interesting passage in the Old Testament. Elijah was told by God to anoint Elisha as a prophet to succeed him. [1 Kings 19:16] So, Elijah does as told, and threw his cloak over Elisha; a sign of transferring mantles. [1 Kings 19:19] Elisha wants to run and tell his family goodbye. [1 Kings 19:20] The response was interesting,

> *"Go back, Elijah replied. What have I done to you."* [1 Kings 19:20]

When Elijah said, "*What have I done to you*," he was essentially saying Elisha's normal living was over. He would no longer live like everyone else. Although Elisha didn't realize it yet, his life was going to be one big battle. As a prophet, he was to be a living, breathing reminder of God to the rebellious house of Israel.

The more a believer becomes a man or a woman of the Spirit [John 16:13], the greater the opposition and friction with the world. Jesus experienced conflict and suffering throughout his entire earthly ministry.

Why the exposition on truth? People who are self-righteous recognize and utilize godly standards. In other words, self-righteous people embrace mid-level truth. They are religious. In general, self-righteous people are proud people who stay "in between the lines." Self-righteousness is rooted in pride. A premium is placed on respectability and image. Godliness is a means to a personal end. It works the letter of the law while ignoring the spirit of the law, or the meaning behind the law.

Life is weighed in relation to others, and if the balance tips towards success, accomplishment, money, better-than, bigger, or position, then the self-righteous person is good enough. However, there is no bell curve because God is the standard, and we all fail. [Romans 3:23]

Jesus told a revealing parable in Luke 18:9-14. It says,

> *To some who were confident of their own righteousness and looked down on everybody else, Jesus told this parable: Two men went up to the temple to pray, one a Pharisee and the other a tax collector. The Pharisee stood up and prayed about himself: God, I thank you that I am not like other men – robbers, evildoers, adulterers – or even like this tax collector. I fast twice a week and give a tenth of all I get. But the tax collector stood at a distance. He would not even look up to heaven, but beat his breast and said, God, have mercy on me, a sinner. I tell you that this man, rather than the other, went home justified before God. For every-one who exalts himself will be humbled, and he who humbles himself will be exalted.*

I knew a woman who was unable to get pregnant. She said, "I haven't slept around, or done drugs like those other women, but they get pregnant." She was a self-righteous person. Her attitude was, "I'm better than them. I deserve to have children."

For me, self-righteousness was a hard lesson. At one point in my life, I really thought I had it going on; a good marriage, a house, two car garage, a new car, money, education, travel, health, respected, a growing church, friends and family. My view was, if a person was lacking, they needed to suck it up, and try harder. Exert your will. God in His infinite mercy humbled me.

As I stated earlier, I lost everything except my

family. My life was turned inside out. I started living off a motorcycle, became promiscuous, drank, and smoked. I came to the realization that I was no better than anyone else. Whatever I had, possessed, or attained in life was simply due to the goodness and kindness of the Lord. [James 1:17]

Recently, I had an interesting conversation with a close friend. He read 2 Timothy and came across the passage,

> "*...having a form of godliness but denying its power.*" [2 Timothy 3:5]

He accurately pointed out that Christians had historically butchered this verse. Believers consistently quote this passage when they feel signs and wonders are lacking. Giftings are vital to healthy body life, and should be emphasized. However, when read contextually, verse 5 has a much different meaning,

> *But mark this: There will be terrible times in the last days. People will be lovers of themselves, lovers of money, boastful, proud, abusive, disobedient to their parents, ungrateful, unholy, without love, unforgiving, slanderous, without self-control, brutal, not lovers of the good, treacherous, rash, conceited, lovers of pleasure rather than lovers of God – having a form of godliness but denying its power. Have nothing to do with them.*
> [2 Timothy 3:1-5]

Within the scope of this passage, power addresses the ability to transform character and behavior. Without the power of God, *people will be lovers of themselves.* At one point in my life, I thirsted and lusted for greater miracles; the dead raised to life, limbs grown, and eyes and ears opened. Now, I'm convinced, the greatest miracles are believers truly walking in Christ's love and humility. I've met a handful of these folks, and I know more are coming with the closing of the age. The beauty is I'm witnessing signs and wonders too.

A fifth major hindrance is sin consciousness. When Adam and Eve sinned in the Garden of Eden, they pulled away from God. [Genesis 3:1-13] Believers do the same. There are three main components to a sin consciousness. The first component is shame. Scripture says Adam and Eve sewed fig leaves together and covered themselves. [Genesis 3:7] Shame conceals or covers. Physical and sexual sin is especially tied to shame. The fruit is embarrassment. A person's image is broken. Believers think to themselves, "if they really knew, what would they think of me?" People are convinced others would condemn them outright. They reason, "if people would reject me, how much more a holy God." People try and sweep away or conceal their sin. The more they focus on their sin, the more they do it. Believers know God knows, and that's why they stay away from Him. Instead of a slip up or a momentary lapse in judgment, believers establish a life-style of sin. They feel trapped, and they are trapped.

Fear is next. After Adam and Eve sinned, they heard God walking in the Garden and hid. [Genesis 3:8] Fear hides. Fear retreats. Proverbs 28:1 says,

> *The wicked man flees though no one pursues, but the righteous are as bold as a lion.*

A fearful person is fully aware of their wrongdoing. I John 4:18 states *"...fear has to do with punishment."* So why do criminals run? They know punishment awaits them. Panic attacks and anxiety are rooted in fear. There is a brooding sense of "here it comes again." Folks feel they deserve punishment because deep down they know what kind of a person they are inside.

Fear swings the other way too. Fear produces inaction and silence. Have you ever felt paralyzed, unable to move? Fear gripped your heart. It seemingly afflicts the spirit or the heart of a person. Show me a person who lacks confidence, and I'll show you a fearful person. Ultimately, what a person fears, dominates them. If a person fears their spouse, he will abuse her. If they fear flying, their life is mapped out according to where they can drive. This is sin fear. It rules and dictates life.

Sinful fear is rooted in pride. Pride deafens. Try reasoning with a proud person. A proud person can't hear. Fear is self-focused and self-centered. So often, counselors coddle and boo-hoo fearful people. Yet, as a person comes to a deeper revelation, fear is the flip side or "heads-up" to pride. Fear is the fruit of pride. Scripture says,

> *God opposes the proud but gives grace to the humble. Submit yourselves, then, to God. Resist the devil, and he will flee from you. Come near to God and he will come near to you. Wash your hands, you sinners, and purify your hearts, you double-minded. Grieve, mourn and wail. Change your laughter to gloom. Humble yourselves before the Lord, and he will lift you up.*
> [James 4:6-10]

When a person walks in sinful fear, they insinuate; the devil, this person, situation, or problem is bigger or greater than God. That is supreme arrogance. Conversely, godly fear is rooted in love. As a person is exposed to the love of God, they begin to see God for who He is. The bible says,

> *But because of his great love for us, God, who is rich in mercy, made us alive with Christ even when we were dead in transgressions – it is by grace you have been saved. And God raised us up with Christ and seated us with him in the heavenly realms in Christ Jesus, in order that in the coming ages he might show the incomparable riches of his grace, expressed in his kindness to us in Christ Jesus. For it is by grace you have been saved, through faith – and this not from yourselves, it is the gift of God – not by works, so that no one can boast.* [Ephesians 2:4-9]

As the believer beholds the Lord, they are captivated, but they're also overwhelmed. It is a fearful thing to behold the Lord. Awe and reverence are all consuming. Mike Bickle asserted that the apostle Paul was not a superhuman Christian; rather, he had a greater revelation of God than do most believers. [Bickle] Revelation changes you. Paul worked out his salvation with fear and trembling. [Philippians 2:12] For many believers, love and fear are paradoxical. Yet, the paradox is a reality. The more believers mature, the more they are able to live with paradox. Maturity lays hold of one truth, while not letting go of the other seemingly contradictory truth.

Finally, there is guilt. In the Fall story, God is looking for Adam, and calls out to him. [Genesis 3:9] Adam responds,

> *"I heard you in the garden, and I was afraid because I was naked; so I hid."* [Genesis 3:10]

God knows what they did, nevertheless, He asks Adam if he ate from the forbidden tree. [vs 11] The response is telling. It reads,

> *The man said, The woman you put here with me---she gave me some fruit from the tree, and I ate it. Then the Lord God said to the woman, What is this you have done? The woman said, The serpent deceived me, and I ate.* [Genesis 3:12-13]

Adam and Eve each placed the blame elsewhere; Adam on God and Eve, and Eve on the serpent. A sure sign of guilt is blame. Whenever there is finger pointing, there is guilt. Guilt is nothing more than a conscious, dreadful awareness of wrong.

The court system is predicated on guilt. When a person violates law, they are guilty. Guilt fuels shame and fear. A person feels ashamed because of what they did. They are afraid because of what they did. For this reason, it is often easier to minister to an outlaw than a church-going deacon. An outlaw's sin is blatant, but a deacon's sin may be subtle. Jesus said,

> *...I tell you the truth, the tax collectors and the prostitutes are entering the kingdom of God ahead of you. For John came to you to show you the way of righteousness, and you did not believe him, but the tax collectors and the prostitutes did. And even after you*

> *saw this, you did not repent and believe him.* [Matthew 21:31-32]

To have a right relationship with God, each person must face their own sin. Bankrupt, broken people are more honest and frank than religious power brokers. Everyone possesses a sense of right and wrong, and therefore, everyone experiences guilt. Guilt blinds. Scripture says in 2 Peter 1:5-9,

> *For this very reason, make every effort to add to your faith goodness; and to goodness, knowledge; and to knowledge, self-control; and to self-control, perseverance; and to perseverance godliness; and to godliness, brotherly kindness; and to brotherly kindness, love. For if you possess these qualities in increasing measure, they will keep you from being ineffective and unproductive in your knowledge of our Lord Jesus Christ. But if anyone does not have them, he is nearsighted and blind, and has forgotten that he has been cleansed from his past sins.*

The implications are if a person possesses a guilty conscious, and focuses on past sins, then, they are unable to grow and mature in Christ. A guilty conscious dims spiritual sight causing blindness. [vs 9] Jesus referred to the Pharisees as blind guides. [Matthew 23:16] The Pharisees attempted to relieve spiritual guilt through strict religious ceremony. As leaders, they expected others to do the same. Their sick, guilt laden hearts blinded them. So much so, that when Jesus stood before them, they couldn't recognize Him. [John 5:39] How blind are we?

The sixth roadblock is idolatry. Most western believers don't view themselves as idolatrous. Western believers think of idolatry as primitive, and associate it with stick and stones of uncivilized, backward people. Yet, idolatry is just as strong in western culture as anywhere else in the world. The Ten Commandments continue to stand the test of time. The Second Commandment reads,

> *You shall not make for yourself an idol in the form of anything in heaven above or on the earth beneath or in the waters below. You shall not bow down to them or worship them; for I, the Lord your God, am a jealous God, punishing the children for the sin of the fathers to the third and fourth generation of those who hate me, but showing love to a thousand generations of those who love me and keep my commandments.* [Exodus 20:4-6]

And, the First Commandment says, *"You shall have no other gods before me."* [Exodus 20:3] Idolatry is the physical manifestation or representation of the god a person worships.

When ancient Israelites fell into idolatry, they worshipped Baal. He was the Canaanite god of fertility, and was often depicted as a bull; bulls impregnate heifers or cows. This pagan god was viewed as the source of rain, which was extremely important to ancient agrarian peoples. Baal rained and impregnated the earth.

To the enlightened western mind, these belief systems appear backward and superstitious. However, don't we do the same thing? The numbers in a bank account determine the wellbeing of most people. What's the difference? The ancient Israelites trusted Baal and rain, and today, people trust money. Jesus said, "*You cannot serve both God and money.*" [Matthew 6:24]

One of the strongest criticisms against the western church has been its lack of power. Maybe, the problem is simply idolatry. Today, quality of living factors in health care. Hospitals are ranked. In some cities, a person can't travel a block without seeing a Walgreen's or a Rite Aid store. Many folks determine where they're going to live, and what they're going to do based on health care. Don't get me wrong. Occasionally, I've received medical attention, and I'm very thankful for the excellent service I received. Even so, my life doesn't revolve around pharmacies or hospitals.

Idolatry is not confined to money and health. I've known gang members who killed another person because of a number or color the victim wore. A good indication of one's allegiance, and therefore love, is what they talk about. That's what they love. Do they talk about the good old days, the club, their kids, motorcycles, or a boyfriend? Jesus said,

> "*For where your treasure is, there your heart will be also.*" [Matthew 6:21]

Once again, things and people are okay, as long as God is supreme. The problem is we not only lie to others but we lie to ourselves.

In my first relationship, my wife had a deadly disease. I told God, "If you heal her, I will serve you all the days of my life." He did. Later, God called me on my promise. My relationship with her did not last. Would I still serve him? I have, albeit, at times reluctantly. He is faithful even when I'm faithless. [2 Timothy 2:13] She was an idol in my heart.

Abraham was extraordinary man, and is known as the father of our faith. [Romans 9:8] He was willing to sacrifice Isaac, his only son, in obedience to God. [Genesis 22:9-12] Father Abraham loved God more than Isaac.

I would caution believers the next time they flippantly judge a biblical character. The vast majority of biblical characters were extraordinary men and women who, even in failure, walked in great courage, faith, and love. If a person takes a serious life inventory, they probably won't be as quick to judge. Jesus said,

> *Do not judge, and you will not be judged. Do not condemn, and you will not be condemned. Forgive, and you will be forgiven. Give and it will be given to you. A good measure, pressed down, and shaken together and running over, will be poured into your lap. For with the measure you use, it will be measured to you.*
> [Luke 6:37-38]

Another idol was my motorcycle. People asked me if I had a girlfriend or a wife, and I responded, "Yah, her name is Dyna. (This is a series of Harley Davidson motorcycles). I treated my bike like a beautiful woman. I parked my bike in the kitchen or the living room. She received great care. We went everywhere together. God called me on this idol too. I sold Dyna, and when I did, I cried.

Few believers understand, or will they ever fully grasp the love of God. God loves us so much that whatever stands between us and Him, He tears down. Believers attribute their misfortune or difficulties to the devil. They make themselves out to be something they're not. Believers naively view themselves as the last bastion of righteousness or the lone prophet of truth, and supposedly, principalities and powers are working day and night for their downfall. More than likely, however, the heavenly Father has pursued them, like a ravenous lion, because He loves them beyond their wildest imagination. No idol, no person, no angel, no money, no fame, no ministry, no devil, no career, no sin is going to keep God from getting to them. Paul said,

> *For I am convinced that neither angels nor demons, neither the present nor the future, nor any powers, neither height nor depth, nor anything else in all of creation, will be able to separate us from the love of God that is in Christ Jesus our Lord.*
> [Romans 8:38-39]

Overwhelming, isn't it?

For a person to overcome their heart, they must first realize, they can't do it. If a person could, they would have already changed. We all need God. He is the only one who can transform people. As David said,

> "*Create in me a pure heart, O God, and renew a steadfast spirit within me.*"
> [Psalm 51:10]

Here's what to do: Find a quiet, secluded place. Get alone with God. It might be bedroom or a mountain top. The location really makes little difference. The important thing is being alone; alone with God.

Next, pour your heart out to God. Everything. When I say everything, I mean everything; events and circumstances you thought you could never tell anyone, what happened as a child, hurts, what you're angry about, who's wronged you, etc. Tell Him how you feel. Speak audibly to God. Don't think it, but once again, speak audibly. Hide nothing. The Psalmist said,

> *"Would not God have discovered it, since he knows the secrets of the heart?"* [Psalm 44:21]

God already knows everything you're telling Him. The difference is you've humbled yourself by sharing your heart. Jesus said,

> *Here I am! I stand at the door and knock. If anyone hears my voice and opens the door, I will come in and eat with him, and he with me.* [Revelation 3:20]

God has waited for you. Empty yourself, everything. Get all the pain out. You should feel better.

A critical step comes now. Confess your sins to God; what you've done wrong. Again, speak audibly. If you start using words like *but* and *because*, stop! You're making excuses. Take ownership for your sins, regardless of others. Each person is responsible for themselves. Tell God the details too. If you're unsure whether something is sin or not, ask Him. You may or may not hear an audible voice, but nevertheless, you'll know. Your spirit will recognize His voice, and give you revelation. A picture or impression might come to mind. You may recall an event. A sensation in your body could trigger a memory. This is God speaking. It is Spirit talk. Just be sensitive, and go with the Spirit. He speaks to you in such a way that you understand. God knows you best. If you have a sense that you did something wrong, you probably did. Confess the sin. Turn over every stone; whatever comes to mind. Know this, God is pleased with you! Jesus Christ died for the forgiveness of your sins.

Whether you realize it or not, you are being

transformed. God is doing something you've never been able to do; purify your heart. You probably feel a little strange. I'm sure you're exhausted too. God loves you so much. He is pleased with you. Worship Him. Tell God how much you love Him. Thank Him. Let Jesus Christ be Lord. You're on the way to freedom. Sleep on it.

James 5:16 says,

> *Therefore confess your sins to each other and pray for each other so that you may be healed.*

Few of us take this passage seriously. Little confession goes on in church. People are proud, and therefore, extremely fearful of exposure. Rather than confessing their sins and being made whole and healthy, people choose a façade with sickness and disease, and sometimes death.

Here's your next step. Confess your sins to someone; "all" your sins. Preferably, this person is the same gender, and older. Pray, and ask God who and He will show you. You may know this person, or, they might be a complete stranger. Sound terrifying? This step is freeing.

Eventually, confession becomes a life-style. You might think to yourself, "You don't know what I've done." I've heard it all: adultery, incest, murder, bestiality, abortion, drugs, crime, prostitution, homosexuality, lying, hustling, abuse, and more. I've sinned, and I've sinned hard. The person the Lord directs you too can handle your confession. As people confessed to me, rarely after a day can I remember any of their confession.

After confession, get baptized. Don't wait! You don't need a six-week course on baptism at the local church. You don't need a certificate. Perhaps you've been baptized before. My advice, do it again. Why? Baptism is about a repentant heart, and not formality or doctrine. You faced the evil in your heart first and foremost with God, and secondly with man. A pool, a bathtub, a spa, a lake, a river, even a canal will do. As you go under the water you're symbolically saying, "I'm leaving my old life behind." When you come up, and out of the water, you are saying, "I'm living for God."

If possible, right your wrongs to the best of your ability. If you need to call someone and apologize, or ask for forgiveness, call. If you need to repay someone, repay. Occasionally, engaging a person from the past could be hurtful to them or someone else. If this is the case, leave it alone. Trust the Lord. The purpose in asking forgiveness and seeking restitution is to bring healing and life to those harmed. Once again, if contact further damages someone's life, don't contact them.

At this stage, you're almost feeling high. You should. This is the freest you've ever been. Jesus said,

> *...I tell you the truth, everyone who sins is a slave to sin. Now a slave has no permanent place in the family, but a son belongs to it forever. So if the Son sets you free, you will be free indeed.* [John 8:34-36]

Since dumping your sin, life is clearer. The world looks brighter. Situations that previously confused you, or seemed hazy are coming into focus. Remember, pride deafens, and guilt blinds. You're free because Jesus set you free.

You are on the path of life, but don't stop. Sunday morning church will not address certain needs in your life. I have nothing against traditional church. In fact, if you know of a good one, go. However, if you want to continue to be transformed into the image of Christ [2 Corinthians 3:18], which you do, then you need more.

More constitutes a small, intimate group of believers coming together, building relationships, moving in gifts, and speaking into each other's lives. This group becomes extended family. New relationships are formed. Your new friends will support and encourage you, and you'll do the same for them. A couple of folks will probably "father" and "mother" you in the things of the Lord. Personal interaction occurs. In traditional settings, you stare at the back of someone's head, and listen to a forty five minute sermon. Participation leads to growth. A small setting affords the opportunity to function in spiritual giftings. Whether you know it or not, you have spiritual gifts. The problem is, like most believers, you have never been given the opportunity to use them.

Fish swim and birds fly. It's natural. If God created you to prophesy, then prophesy. If He created you to serve food, then serve. Generally speaking, traditional church ministry is limited to four or five areas; greeting and ushering, administration, teaching Sunday school, and music or worship. If your niche is one of these ministries, that's wonderful. However, you still need interactive relationships. Don't get pigeon holed.

When believers attempt to do things they're not called to, they get frustrated, and frustrate those around them. Your new family will draw your calling out. Ministry is natural and fulfilling, and others affirm you. Moreover, character issues are addressed and corrected here too. You can only work through character issues in family settings. House churches are good. Some people attend relational gatherings. Others prefer cell groups. Ask around, they're everywhere. Go online. I think you'll be surprised at what's out there.

Few people have the fortitude to do what you've just done. If you followed the previous steps, your life will never be the same. Aside from water baptism, you will repeat those steps throughout your life. You're not just recovering, or even surviving, you are overcoming, and therefore, you are an overcomer. Since you've chosen to clean your heart up, everything changes. God is radically restructuring your life.

MEN

I had a dream
But it turned to dust
What I thought was love
That must have been lust
SANTANA *WINNING*

Before I delve into a discussion about men, more groundwork needs to be established. There are three areas of consideration which consistently cause confusion amongst believers, and affect the remainder of our discussion. These areas are the western worldview, roles and functions, and relationships.

Everyone is culturally indoctrinated. People are influenced by their experiences. They are born and raised in a unique set of circumstances. We can never completely divest ourselves from our cultural contexts. As a result, many people think to themselves, "This is the way life is supposed to be." Yet, virtually no one would argue that life in urban Calcutta is vastly different from life in rural Nebraska. What's normal?

For believers, whether they live in Nigeria or the Netherlands, the bible is the ultimate standard. Biblical writers wrote from an eastern, Hebraic mindset or worldview. Hebraic thought clashes on a few very important points with the western mindset. Don't get me wrong, western thinking led to the scientific revolution, and has paid huge dividends. Even now, I'm typing away on a computer that is the direct result of western ingenuity. I enjoy my iPod, flat screen, and microwave too. Even so, toys and conveniences are not the end-all.

The western worldview is entrenched in ancient Greek and Roman thought. The ancients thought vertically and top-down. Life was structured according to tiers of title, rank and superiority. Their pantheon of gods had spheres of power; some greater and some lesser. In other words, there was a distinct pecking order. If a person mapped out the structure of the gods as well as ancient government and culture, it would look like a pyramid. The West adopted Aristotelian philosophy by using sets and subsets to categorically organize.

Conversely, the eastern/Hebraic worldview is organic and fluid. Rather than vertical and linear, life is horizontal and cyclical. Instead of rank and superiority, Hebrew thought embraces responsibility and servanthood. Relationship is a key value. Life is an overlapping, interconnected whole.

Reflect momentarily. Consider government, business, and even education. Obviously, the western worldview predominates the West. However, these thoughts also spilled over into Christendom. As I stated earlier, western culture influenced Christianity more than Christianity influenced western culture. Churches are structured like secular government and businesses, top-down.

In order to possess a tax-exempt status, churches are required to have a constitution. Ministers resemble kind, caring bosses. Parishioners, like good employees, work hard at fulfilling the vision of the minister. To rise in the church means to acquire a title, and have people working for you.

People attend church to satisfy ultimate questions. If churches model government and business, then the people attending are directly influenced. Believers buy into church values. In turn, their homes and relationships are patterned after the same ideology and values.

As title and superiority is to western thought, so is role and function to God's kingdom. When a police chief or a surgeon speaks, their words carry clout. The title and position implies authority. People immediately associate the designation with superiority and veracity. To arrive at such a position, the person must be an expert. Right?

Scripture challenges believers to a much different standard. Romans 12:2 says,

> *"Do not conform any longer to the pattern of this world..."*

And Romans 12:4-5 says,

> *Just as each of us has one body with many members, and these members do not all have the same function, so in Christ we who are many form one body, and each member belongs to all the others.*

The pattern of the world is to attain a title or a position of superiority. Yet, nowhere in scripture does it say we are better than anyone else. If anything, we are to consider others better than ourselves. [Philippians 2:3] Paul likened the role and function of the believer to the natural body. The eye functions by seeing. The ear functions by hearing. My eyes and ears are not jockeying for dominance. They simply conform to their design and purpose. The reality is each body part serves and compliments the others.

A person's role is who they are and their function is how they act out that role. Peter and John were both apostles (roles). Peter was in the forefront, spoke up and evangelized (function). John was supportive, a lover, and prayed for extended periods of time (function).

There is symmetry throughout God's creation. Roles and functions apply to genders too. Men have a role and women have a role. How each individual functions is determined by a multitude of factors; upbringing, culture, giftings and talents, experiences, passions, personality, and even genetics.

As much as anything, however, our roles and functions are contingent upon relationships. Our gracious God blesses each individual with a number of gifts and talents. Everyone possesses something innately great. Proper relationship is required for that greatness to shine forth. A man might be a wonderful husband and father, but until he marries a woman and has children, those traits are mere possibilities. Improper relationships retard one's greatness too. Have you ever watched a professional athlete struggle, and when they're traded to another team, they become a superstar? Consider Jesus. As he returned to his hometown, everyone saw him as a carpenter rather than as a prophet or the Christ. Since people related to him as a carpenter, *"He could not do any great miracles there."* [Mark 6:5] Unless folks are correctly aligned, callings and purpose are stifled.

In summary, the church, and therefore believers, has embraced a western worldview. Church is structured like a pyramid with top-down, hierarchal positions, rather than roles and functions. Unless believers return to biblical standards, and enter into proper relationships, they will fail to realize God's best for themselves and others.

Each gender possesses nobility and grace. Men and women together complete the image of God. Nevertheless, there are benchmarks or qualities that distinguish men. These are authority, fatherhood, sacrificial love, intercession, and purpose.

Genesis 2:19-20 says,

Now the Lord God had formed out of the ground all the beasts of the field and all the birds of the air. He brought them to the man to see what he would name them; and whatever the man called each living creature, that was its name. So the man gave names to all the livestock, the birds of the air and all the beasts of the field.

Adam was supernaturally articulate and intelligent. Scientists spend their entire lives attempting to categorize and understand just one species. Adam named them all. If Adam is compared with men today, sin has devastated our intelligence. There is a deeper, richer revelation here though. When someone names something, they are exercising authority. Within the Hebrew understanding, naming was not just confined to identity, but also set in motion purpose and destiny. Adam defined his world. He exercised his authority. Scripture says,

God blessed them and said to them, Be fruitful and increase in number; fill the earth and subdue it. Rule over the fish of the sea and the birds of the air and over every living creature that moves on the ground. [Genesis 1:28]

Adam named his wife Eve meaning "living." [Genesis 3:20] Eventually, she became the mother of all humankind. Words are powerful. The well used passage in Proverbs 18:21 says,

"The tongue has the power of life and death, and those who love it will eat its fruit."

On a couple of different occasions, I worked for Christian companies. At one company, a group of us prayed together weekly. We prayed for each other's needs. A coworker had an abusive husband; he boozed and womanized. Each week she brought a new horror story. We constantly asked God to change his heart. After a few months, I was fed up. I said with great fervency and passion, "Lord, break his heart." That afternoon, he was rushed to the hospital with a massive heart attack. Spoken words come to pass.

Today, naming children is routinely left to mothers. Meanings are ignored, and instead, trendy names are chosen. Movies and sit-coms influence parents more than heritage and scripture. The biblical example is different. Father Abraham named his son Isaac. [Genesis 21:3] Zechariah named his son John according to the word spoken by the archangel Gabriel. [Luke 1:13] Even our heavenly Father selected His son's name. Jesus is the Greek form of the Hebrew Jeshua which means "He will save." [Jackson 52]

A name can inspire a destiny. I was named Walter after my deceased grandfather. Walter is Germanic, and means "powerful warrior." Even before I was born, I had a distinct sense of communing with the Lord in my mother's womb. As a little boy, I remember numerous spiritual encounters, both good and evil. Over the years I've flowed in discerning of spirits and prophesy.
I derive great joy from seeing people healed and delivered, and stepping into their calling and purpose. As my name implies, I've warred for myself and others.

Men must embrace their authority. Naming children is a God-given function. Names start destinies.

What is authority? Luke 4:32 says of Jesus,

> *"They were amazed at his teaching,*
> *because his message had authority."*

And, Matthew 9:4-7 says,

> *Knowing their thoughts, Jesus said, Why do you entertain evil thoughts in your hearts? Which is easier: to say, Your sins are forgiven, or to say, Get up and walk? But so that you may know that the Son of Man has authority on earth to forgive sin... Then he said to the paralytic, Get up, take your mat and go home. And the man got up and went home.*

People recognized authority in Jesus, and sin or sickness submitted to him. Where did his authority come from? Jesus says,

> *For as the Father has life in himself, so he has granted the Son to have life in himself. And he has given him authority to judge because he is the Son of Man.* [John 5:26-27]

Jesus' authority came from God. The Father endorsed and backed His Son. By being God's Son, Jesus spoke on behalf of his Father. His words and actions represented God. A simple, but accurate definition of authority is: the power to enforce values. When people heard Jesus, they were moved. Why? God spoke through Jesus. Perhaps not everyone embraced his message, nevertheless, at the very least, everyone knew his words were weighty and possessed authority. Sickness submitted because Jesus carried heaven's endorsement. He influenced and changed life wherever he went. God showed up when Jesus showed up.

Originally, men were to exercise God-endorsed

authority on earth. What Jesus did, men are to do! He modeled the transcendent norm, not the exception.

Sin caused Adam's authority to short-circuit, and since then, every other man has sinned too. Adam broke God's commandment by eating from the forbidden tree. [Genesis 3:17] Scripture says,

> *For since death came through a man, the resurrection of the dead comes also through a man. For as in Adam all die, so as in Christ all will be made alive.*
> [1 Corinthians 15:21-22]

Men lose authority when they sin. Power is authority in action. This is why Jesus walked and lived in such pure, heavenly authority and power. He was without sin. [Hebrews 4:15] Sin retards authority; which means, men don't have power to enforce God's values. A few men may contend, "It's not my righteousness but the righteousness of Christ." [Romans 3:22] They are absolutely right. However, scripture also says,

> *No one who is born of God will continue to sin, because God's seed remains in him; he cannot go on sinning, because he has been born of God. This is how we know who the children of God are and who the children of the devil are: Anyone who does not do what is right is not a child of God; nor is anyone who does not love his brother.*
> [1 John 3:9-10]

Stop sinning! If a man wants to see his family healthy and whole, it starts in his heart. His holiness will affect his neighborhood and community too. A godly man will have authority over the elements, sickness and disease, and even dark powers. But he must walk in purity. Father,

> *"...Your kingdom come, your will be done on earth as it is in heaven."* [Matthew 6:10]

A close woman friend asked, "Aren't women suppose to walk in great authority too?" Yes. To be sure, scripture is very clear; Adam and Eve co-ruled. [Genesis 1:28] However, God placed men in one role, and women in another role. Scripture says,

> *Now I want you to realize that the head of every man is Christ, and the head of the woman is man, and the head of Christ is God.* [1 Corinthians 11:3]

There is divine order. It goes on to say,

> *A man ought not to cover his head, since he is the image and glory of God; but the woman is the glory of man. For man did not come from woman, but woman from man; neither was man created for woman, but woman for man.* [1 Corinthians 11:7-9]

Since men are placed in a position of headship, there is greater responsibility, which in turn, translates into greater authority. Superiority is not a factor, or even a consideration. God created men to do one thing, and women to do something else. With greater responsibility, also comes greater consequence. In James 3:1 it says,

> *Not many of you should presume to be teachers, my brothers, because you know that we who teach will be judged more strictly.*

God makes teachers, and they must accept their responsibility. God makes men, and they must accept their responsibility too. In the Garden, Eve sinned first. [Genesis 3:7] Yet, even so, sin did not enter the world. Sin came into the world through one man, Adam. [Romans 5:12] God told Adam, specifically, the ground is cursed because of you. [Genesis 3:17]

Years ago, a rock hit the windshield of my car. The rock made a tiny chip or divot in the glass. Springtime arrived, and we had one of those days which was cold in the morning, and hot in the afternoon. My little chip turned into a huge crack that ruined my entire windshield. Adam's sin did the same thing; it spread throughout creation.

I remember an interesting story. A young woman struggled in a particular area of her life. She lived on the other side of the country from her family. The mother faithfully prayed for the young woman. The struggle continued though. One night, the mother received a revelation that the father, as the head of the household, needed to take authority over a demonic intruder working in their daughter's life.

The following day, the mother and father phoned the daughter, and the father rebuked the demonic intruder. The young woman convulsed, a spirit immediately left her, scurried across the floor, and out of the house. When there is proper alignment, men function in their masculinity, or according to their role. In turn, women will function in their femininity. It's natural. Maleness leads to masculinity. Masculinity leads to manliness. Eventually, manliness matures into fatherhood.

A while back I had an interesting conversation with the writer and prophet John Moore. [Moore] He felt there was a lack of "manliness" in the body of Christ. I reflected on that statement. I'm convinced he was right.

Once, I invited friends to a conference. The

speaker was promoted as a great prophet of God. Without a doubt, he walked in an extraordinary prophetic gifting. However, his demeanor was extremely feminine. My friends wouldn't come back. Two men were convinced he was homosexual. As I thought of him, Liberace continually came to mind. He reminded me of the late entertainer Liberace. A "Liberace" is not the kind of guy you want watching your back. Manliness was lacking. The issue centers on masculinity. We've watered down distinctions between boys and girls, and men and women. Highlighting similarities is good. However, highlighting distinctions is better.

Here's a challenge. Peruse scripture where roles of men and women are outlined. Distinctions are emphasized, not diluted. Androgyny is as much a perversion as homosexuality or lesbianism. These perversions advocate sameness, and sameness is contrary to God. Even within the Godhead; Father, Son, and Holy Spirit function in unique roles, yet, they're one.

If masculinity is not cultivated and celebrated in homes, we will never get men. Ministers and parents love to quote the verse,

> *"Train a child in the way he should go, and when he is old he will not turn from it."*
> *[Proverbs 22:6]*

Generally, the interpretation is confined to hope and trusting God; the prodigal returns to the faith after a season of waywardness. The passage includes this interpretation, but it is also far more expansive. Godly training must include one's role in life. Training boys means modeling manliness. A number of cultures celebrate the passage from boyhood to manhood. In the West, we lack these rites of passage. Many men are boys in men's bodies.

Their masculinity was never nurtured, and though they matured physically and even mentally, they certainly never matured spiritually. As a result, we have few fathers. Fatherhood is the natural outgrowth of manliness. Malachi 4:6 says,

> *He will turn the hearts of the fathers to their children, and the hearts of the children to the fathers; or else I will come and strike the land with a curse.*

In Luke 1:17, the thought is expressed slightly different,

> *And he will go on before the Lord, in the spirit and power of Elijah, to turn the hearts of the fathers to their children and the disobedient to the wisdom of the righteous – to make ready a people prepared for the Lord.*

He refers to the one who comes in the power and spirit of Elijah. The passages allude to, or indicate that unless the hearts of the fathers turn towards the children, the children will not embrace righteousness. If the turning of hearts doesn't occur, God will strike the land with a curse. Read the papers. Go online. The curse is here. Isaiah 3:12 says,

> *Youths oppress my people, women rule over them. O my people, your guides lead you astray; they turn you from the path.*

Rings true, doesn't it? The whole order is skewed. The term "fathers" used in the previous passages means exactly that, fathers. The reference is not alluding to seniors, or males and females over thirty, but specifically fathers.

I worked a number of years in a boy's group home.

Three factors or common problems consistently affected the boys awarded to us by the courts. One, these boys were affiliated to one degree or another with a gang. Secondly, the vast majority used drugs. These days, the drug of choice is methamphetamines. Thirdly, and most importantly, these kids were virtually always fatherless. Without a father, children, and in particular boys, search for identity through other avenues.

Like a lot of believers, I skip through genealogies while reading the bible. Yet, there is an important principle here. In scripture, genealogies say something like, "the son of," or "the father of." Father's provide an identity or heritage, or a clan or a tribe; a place of belonging. Young, fatherless girls become promiscuous because the same need and desire rushes through their hearts.

The church struggles here too. Paul said,

> *Even though you have ten thousand guardians in Christ, you do not have many fathers...* [1 Corinthians 4:15]

Much of the present day rebellion and inner turmoil in churches is due to the lack of spiritual fathers. Fathers stabilize. As I reflect over my own spiritual journey, I can honestly say, I've never had a spiritual father in the church. I've had spiritual mothers, but not fathers. A few years back, I organized conferences in the community where I lived. I consistently brought in a particular teacher. Gradually, he became something of a spiritual father to me. Things crumbled though. And really, as I've said all along, the problem was me. Once the conferences stopped, and I wasn't putting two thousand dollars in his hand anymore, I never heard from him again.

When life gets hard, and even ugly, a person quickly finds out who their friends are, and who isn't a friend. I learned. God dealt with my heart. Regardless of my church experience, I know what true fatherhood is all about. My biological father is the genuine article. No matter what's happened in my life, even when I'm to blame, he is always there for me. My friends seek him out too. I am the most blessed of men.

Paul said in Romans 7:15-23,

> *I do not understand what I do. For what I want to do I do not do, but what I hate to do. And if I do what I do not want to do, I agree that the law is good. As it is, it is no longer I myself who do it, but the sin living in me. I know that nothing good lives in me, that is, my sinful nature. For I have the desire to do good, but I cannot carry it out. For what I do is not the good I want to do; no, the evil I do not want to do – this I keep on doing. Now if I do what I do not want to do, it is no longer I who do it, but it is sin living in me that does it. So I find this law at work: When I want to do good, evil is right there with me. For in my inner being I delight in God's law; but I see another law at work in the members of my body, waging war against the law of my mind and making me a prisoner of the law of sin at work within my members.*

I think most believers can relate to this passage. People struggle in certain areas of their lives. And no matter how hard they try, they just can't get past the struggle. Paul said "*in my inner being I delight in God's law.*" In other words, Paul knows what is godly, and wants to do right. Yet, he goes on to say,

> *...But I see another law at work in the*

> *members of my body, waging war against the law of my mind and making me a prisoner of the law of sin at work within my members.*

So what's going on? I was exposed to a number of ministries as well as secular counseling: deliverance, inner healing, restoring the foundations, theophostic prayer, power ministries, prophetic counsel, healing rooms, twelve-step programs, accountability groups, psychology, psychiatry, and medications. There are no formulas. Believers need the Holy Spirit.

Some poor souls battle over and over again with the same issues. They literally live out the previous passage. Many of them have done all they know to do. A number of ministries take the view that all our problems are spiritual, and many of the "chronic" cases are just rebellious people refusing to give up their sin. Conversely, hard core mental health professionals relegate behavioral problems to basic chemical, physiological imbalances.

An important consideration is overlooked though. Paul referred to "*sinful nature*." Everyone has heard statements like, "Oh, he's just like his father" or "She acts just like her mom." Traits can be identified in grand-children, or even great-grandchildren. Abraham lied about his wife Sarah to protect his own life. [Genesis 20] Isaac, Abraham's son, did the same with his wife Rebekah. [Genesis 26:7-9] Jacob, Abraham's grandson, lied to get the blessing from Isaac. [Genesis 27] Was lying nurtured or valued by Abraham and his descendents? Or was lying in his genes? Nature or Nurture? Genetic or Environment? My gut feeling is most believers would say the patriarchs had serious character defects. They did.

Sin, however, does not simply afflict the soul and spirit. Adam died physically after he sinned. [Genesis 5:5]

Paul also said,

> "*...but I see another law at work in the members of my body....*"

Sin seeps into our cells and flesh too. Each individual cell carries DNA, identifying a person and their ancestors. Today, if one is unsure of their ethnicity or ancestry, they can be tested. By comparing DNA samples, researchers can determine family ties.

Have you ever noticed how different Italians are from English? Mexicans from Scandinavians? DNA is unique. Why do people believe only "good" is passed down genetically? The Irish have the reputation for being the friendliest people in Europe. They are known as serious beer drinkers. Can "friendly" be passed down biologically? "Drunkenness?" Why not? What about fear, anger, or greed? Again, why not? Is behavior confined to environmental factors, or does it exceed that? Human behavior is tangled between nature and nurture. Environmental factors seemingly ignite genetic predispositions; either for the better or for the worse. We are physical beings and this truth cannot be ignored.

Earlier, I said the issues of life flow from the heart. So which is it, spiritual or physical? It is both. Life is whole. A Greek view categorizes and divides. An eastern, Hebraic view integrates and combines. The biological mixes with spirit and soul. There is overlap. Scripture says, "*the blood is the life.*" [Deuteronomy 12:23] Blood carries DNA from parents to children. And, Exodus 20:5 says,

> *...punishing the children for the sin of the fathers to the third and fourth generation of those who hate me...*

Many believers consider curses and blessings like fairy dust; they supernaturally settle on us. If the believer prays hard enough, the fairy dust blows away. I'm convinced curses and blessings are embedded in our genetic makeup. They're in our cells. Paul gives the answer when he says, "*another law at work in the members of my body.*" There is an antidote too. Romans 8:13-14 says,

> *For if you live according to the sinful nature, you will die; but if by the Spirit you put to death the misdeeds of the body, you will live, because those who are led by the Spirit of God are sons of God.*

The Spirit of God puts to death misdeeds of the body. He destroys curses embedded in our cells. Believers need to pray for people's physiological condition, or genetic makeup. Believers who perpetually struggle would get over the hump, so to speak. Normally, ministry is limited to physical healing in terms of restoring bodily functions like hearing, or curing diseases like cancer. But, when the Spirit of God is present, the fabric of life is altered. Moses, as an older man, was full of life because of the presence of the Lord. [Deuteronomy 34:7] Aaron's staff budded. [Hebrews 9:4] When a dead man touched Elisha's bones, he came back to life. [2 Kings 13:21] Paul refers to those who are led by the Spirit as "*sons of God.*" The believer's DNA is divine; full of health, life and power. The effect of our transformation is far more reaching than we presently understand. Paul goes on to say,

> *The creation waits in eager expectation for the sons of God to be revealed. For the*

> *creation was subjected to frustration, not by its own choice, but by the will of the one who subjected it, in hope that the creation itself will be liberated its bondage to decay and brought into the glorious freedom of the children of God.* [Romans 8:19-21]

Some biblical heroes held a special relationship with God. Why? These men were friends of God. One such man was King David. He was a man after God's own heart. [Acts 13:22] It says in 2 Chronicles 14:2,

> *And David knew that the Lord had established him as king over Israel and that his kingdom had been highly exalted for the sake of his people Israel.*

Yes, David had great authority, and he was a father to the people. More than great authority, however, he loved. David deeply loved God's people. God exalted David because He could trust David with Israel. As power is to authority, so intercession is to love. A loving king, like David, went before his people, whether good or bad. He interceded. Even as a youth, David interceded on behalf of Israel. [1 Samuel 17] The story of David and Goliath is one of intervention. He stood between the giant Goliath and God's people. The story is often depicted as good versus evil, or the shepherd boy against the fearsome giant. That's true. At the heart of the matter though, is love. David said,

> "*...Who is this uncircumcised Philistine that he should defy the armies of the living God?*" [1 Samuel 17:26]

David would not allow God's people to be dishonored.

Others were dear to God as well. Abraham was called a friend of God. [2 Chronicles 20:7] He was an intercessor too, and therefore a lover. Abraham knew Sodom and Gomorrah were being evaluated by God, so he immediately interceded and contended for them. [Genesis 18:20-33] Aside from his nephew Lot and his family, there is no reason to assume Abraham had any other meaningful relationships in those communities. Abraham stood between God and Sodom and Gomorrah. [Genesis 18:22] Intercession is fueled by a tender heart filled with love.

Moses, like David and Abraham, was an intercessor. When God was angry with Israel, and sought to destroy them, Moses intervened. [Exodus 32:9-14] The bible says of Moses,

> "*The Lord would speak to Moses face to face, as a man speaks to his friend.*"
> [Exodus 33:11]

Aaron and Miriam, Moses' brother and sister, openly opposed him. God struck Miriam with leprosy. [Numbers 12:10] Immediately, Moses interceded and Miriam was restored. [Numbers 12:13] Moses even loved those who wronged him.

Scripture says of the Fall story,

> *When the woman saw that the fruit of the tree was good for food and pleasing to the eye, and also desirable for gaining wisdom, she took some and ate it. She also gave some to her husband, who was with her, and he ate it.* [Genesis 3:6]

Adam knew better. Before God created Eve, He told Adam,

> *You are free to eat from any tree in the garden; but you must not eat from the tree of knowledge of good and evil, for when you eat of it you will surely die.*
> [Genesis 2:16-17]

We don't know if God ever specifically told Eve not to eat from the forbidden tree. Adam knew full well God's command though, and yet, failed to intercede on behalf of Eve. Even after she ate the fruit, Adam could have still interceded. He was right there with Eve. Because of his role, Adam was responsible for Eve. The design has never changed.

Jesus is our standard. Paul likens the relationship between husbands and wives to Christ and his church. [Ephesians 5:22-33] Scholarship has debated extensively, for years, on what the Ephesians text and other male/female passages really mean. There is a broad spectrum of interpretations. Scripture consistently deals with the heart. Jesus so loved his people that he willingly sacrificed His life on their behalf. [John 10:15] Since then, he continues to intercede for us before the Father. [Romans 8:34] He's been interceding for millennia. Love like this is the mark of a godly man. [1 John 4:7-8]

How seriously does God take intercession? Over the years, I've encountered many prophets and prophetic people. It seems as though everyone called to prophetic ministry is either an Elijah, or a Deborah, or at least those are the words spoken over their lives.

First of all, not everyone is called to this type of ministry. Secondly, many of these folks are simply unhappy and insecure. Men want to be "Elijah" so they can call fire down on someone who opposes them. Bitter, frustrated women want to sit in a position of authority like Deborah. Why aren't there more ministries like Hosea,

John, or Barnabas? Or like Abigail, Lydia, or Anna? The reason is few of us really know the heart of our heavenly Father.

A few years ago, I visited a little independent church one Sunday morning. A gal stared at me. After the service, she walked over to me, and said, "I feel like the Lord wants me to tell you something, 'Mary.' That's all." She then walked off. Well, that word was huge for me. I consider it one of the best words I've received. Because of the season in my life, I purposed in my heart to be like Mary, and sit at the feet of Jesus. I wanted to choose the better. [Luke 10:42] What's the point? The point is I had no problem being like Mary, a woman who loved her Lord and Savior, instead of the stereotypical, spindly, finger pointing, fire-breathing prophet.

Elijah was the consummate prophet of power. He momentarily lapsed, and fled from the wicked queen Jezebel. [1 Kings 19:3] Afterward, God told Elijah he will be replaced by Elisha. [1 Kings 19:16] When I first read that story, I felt God was unfair to Elijah. Who hasn't flipped out, or struggled? A Canadian minister by the name of David Demian clarified the reasoning for me. [Demian] Romans 11:2 says,

> *God did not reject his people, whom he foreknew. Don't you know what the Scripture says in the passage about Elijah – how he appealed to God against Israel...*

The word *appealed*, can be and often is translated as "interceded." Elijah interceded against God's people. As a result, God replaced him. That's how seriously God takes intercession.

In the New Testament, Jesus rebuked James and John because they wanted to call down fire on a Samaritan village. [Luke 9:52-56] The brothers were of the wrong spirit. Finally, Peter instructs husbands to respect their wives, otherwise, the implications are that their prayers will be hindered. [1 Peter 3:7] Where there isn't any respect, there isn't any love. God is love. [1 John 4:16] Men are to love their wives as Christ loves the Church.

Some years ago, a prolific Christian writer wrote a book on spiritual gifts. He believed the majority of intercessors were women. After I dug into Genesis, and read stories about Abraham, Moses and David, the design appears to be men as a gender are called to intercession. Is the decaying family symptomatic of a lack of intercession by men? Divorce? I think so. In fact, spiritually, the body of Christ is handicapped. When the natural body isn't functioning properly, the other parts compensate. For example, if one can't see, the hearing, so I'm told, becomes extremely sensitive and fine tuned to compensate. This is exactly what's happened within the body of Christ. Women have compensated for the lack of intercession by men. Men were made to intercede.

Men need divine purpose too. Scripture says of Adam,

> *The Lord God took the man and put him in the Garden of Eden to work it and take care of it.* [Genesis 2:15]

God assigned Adam a domain or a sphere. Each man needs his own garden. God has a niche for every man. Without purpose, men wander and meander through life. They lack meaning and focus. This was Cain's punishment. After he killed his brother Abel, God said to him, "*You will be a restless wanderer on the earth.*" [Genesis 4:12] And Cain's response was, "*My punishment is more than I can bear.*" [Genesis 4:13]

A tormented man is a man who lacks purpose and

direction. God desires to shoot men like arrows. An arrow or a bullet is dangerous when there is no target; they possess the potential to inadvertently damage something or someone. Men are the same way. Without ordained purpose, men are much more likely to inflict harm. They become misguided and disrupt the lives and spheres of others. How? A man takes a position that was meant for someone else. Or, men attempt to be something they were never designed to be, and in so doing, disrupt a business or an organization from fulfilling its mission. Know God, and in so doing, know your purpose.

Where do men, as a gender, encounter pitfalls? Once again, the answer is found in Genesis. Adam allowed Eve to eat forbidden fruit, and then he ate too. [Genesis 3:6] Why didn't Adam stop Eve? And, why did Adam eat the fruit too, knowing it was evil? Eve listened to the serpent. [Genesis 3:1-4] Adam, however, listened to Eve. [Genesis 3:17] While fully knowing the evil, he passively submitted to Eve. Adam abdicated his role of headship. Since the fall, men continue to abdicate their role of headship.

I'm not insinuating that men shouldn't listen to their wives. Husband and wife relationships are one of mutual submission. That is, each is to respect and listen to the other. Nevertheless, someone needs the final say, and God has designated that role to men. To be quite frank, I've seen few marriages I consider godly. The order is tweaked. Men take the role of women, and women take the role of men. If I talk to men, they say, "She's controlling and manipulative." If I talk to women, they say, "He doesn't do anything, so I have to." In my view, the brunt of the problem is men.

Have you ever ridden horses? If a horse acts up, or gets out of control, pull the reins hard to one side. The horse's head goes in the direction you pull. The body follows. Eventually, the animal settles down, or tires itself out. If the head of the household, men, line up with God, and accept their responsibility, women and the rest of the family will follow. I also believe women will welcome the leadership. Men must stop blaming women, and step into their role of headship.

Adam ate the fruit after his abdication because he was afraid of being alone. Remember, God said,

> *"It is not good for man to be alone. I will make a helper suitable for him."*
> [Genesis 2:18]

Men, by their very nature, are not meant to be alone. Scripture also says,

> *"He who finds a wife finds what is good and receives favor from the Lord."*
> [Proverbs 18:22]

God intended men to have a wife. Scripture infers wives are a blessing from God. Marriage is divine design. Men innately need companionship. It is a need God placed in them, and cannot be repented of, or turned away from.

When I got involved in ministry again, I immediately had kidney stone attacks. If you've never had a kidney stone, thank God. I spoke to a couple of women who passed kidney stones and birthed children. They felt the stones were more painful than the delivery of their children.

The routine went like this: Whenever I went to a ministry function, even enroute, boom! I had excruciating pain. Next, a friend or family member drove me to the physician. I got a shot of Demerol, and spent a day or two coming off the drug and recouping from the pain.

People fasted and prayed for me. I confessed any sin that came to mind. I ate fruits and vegetables, and drank water. I faithfully walked and exercised too. Still, the attacks continued. The attacks were such a regular occurrence that the physician's staff thought I was getting shots just to get high. Eventually, I went to the hospital, and had a scan. Two stones showed up. Then I received my revelation.

One stone represented a wife, and another stone represented a child. In my heart, I felt robbed. I was faithful to a chronically ill, infertile woman. She jerked a little boy out of my life. In my other marriage, the woman underwent a hysterectomy. Both women divorced me, and I felt rejected. But the problem was me. Even God given desires must be submitted to the Lordship of Jesus Christ. My desire for a wife and child interfered with my relationship with the Lord. I got hooked. Yet, my hook or desire was godly.

Have you ever wondered about the bizarre sacrifices in the bible? Old Testament sacrifices took on a whole new meaning for me. Biblically, kidneys are associated with emotions and desires. [Job 16:13] Certain sacrifices required burning the kidneys, and the fat around them. [Leviticus 3 and 4] Fat is symbolic of energy. [Psalms 92:14] Kidneys and fat were burned on the Alter because they represented the selfish desires, efforts, and energies of the one making the sacrifice. Our desires, even godly ones, must be surrendered to the will of the Father. Since my revelation, I haven't had another kidney stone. Many physical conditions and afflictions are nothing more than deep seated spiritual issues. Satan hooked me through godly desires gone awry.

If you ask women what men want, they'll say, almost without exception, "Sex." In a certain respect, they're spot on. Men satiate their desire for companionship with sex. Sex is like eating Big Mac's all the time. Your hunger goes away, but shortly thereafter, you need more. There is little or no nutritional value in fast food. Sex is similar. It feels good, but, it's empty of lasting fulfillment. Men develop promiscuous lifestyles, but, are never satisfied.

Bars provide pseudo-satisfaction. Intimacy is the motivation behind companionship. Men desire someone they can share their innermost feelings and thoughts with, and still be loved. In the bar, "liquid courage" helps men open their hearts. If you want to find out how someone is really doing, sit beside them on a bar stool. Yet, like sex, contentment is fleeting. Barroom talk only goes so far. Alcohol induced conversations are rooted in selfishness, not God. Most addictions can be attributed to broken relationships, isolation, and a lack of intimacy, first and foremost with God, and secondly with others.

Men need intimacy. A godly woman meets that need best. Intimacy between a man and a woman is in His design. Satan twists and distorts God's design, and men comply. Through each distortion, demonic entities gain access. Lust attacks men. Every man, if all his "equipment" works properly, will at some point battle lust. It has been called "every man's disease." Some men blame women in the way they dress and carry themselves. Many women use their femininity to seduce and manipulate men. The problem starts on the inside though. Men are seduced because they want to be seduced. Lustful motives get men what they deserve in the end -- nothing.

Men need other men to hold them accountable. Healthy male friendships provide a venue for sharing sexual struggles. Every man has struggled with lust, and if he says he hasn't, he's a liar. Women won't understand. Testosterone-charged lust lies outside the experience of women.

When I worked in a boy's group home, the boys

ranged in age from thirteen to seventeen. Females, as young as twenty or twenty one year's old worked there too. Young gals, and older women for that matter, have no idea what a young man feels with an erection. It's as ridiculous as me advising women on feminine hygiene products, or how to ease premenstrual symptoms.

Keep boundaries clear. God gave men brothers and fathers and gave women sisters and mothers. That's His order.

WOMEN

Let me be all that I can be
Don't smother me with negativity
Whatever's out there waiting for me
I'm going to face it willingly
JOSS STONE *RIGHT TO BE WRONG*

Women have an equally high-calling to men. The benchmarks distinguishing godly women are servanthood, faithful love, authority, and motherhood. Genesis 2:18 says,

> *The Lord God said, It is not good for the man to be alone. I will make a helper suitable for him.*

Women were created to help men. Service and support are in God's grand design. Scripture also says,

> *Wives submit to your husbands as to the Lord. For the husband is the head of the wife as Christ is the head of the church, his body, of which he is the Savior. Now as the church submits to Christ, so also wives should submit to their husbands in everything.* [Ephesians 5:22-24]

Some women cringe when they hear and read these verses.

Words like *help*, *service* and especially *submission* can carry negative connotations. These words are associated with hurtful relationships. Perhaps a parent, a spouse, or even a boss "lorded" over them. Past abuses have left many women suspicious and guarded, and rightly so.

Conversely, culture dramatically influences us too. Instead of biblical role models like Sarah or Mary, a lot of women emulate Hollywood divas or high powered professionals. Fame and money afford women power similar to the powerful men we've had in western culture for centuries. Rather than getting stepped on and used, powerful women dictate their own terms and conditions.

If someone is at the top, everyone else is below. Superiority insulates one from dangers others have to endure. Values like superiority are worldly though, and not heavenly. Jesus said,

> *You know that the rulers of the Gentiles lord it over them, and their high officials exercise authority over them. Not so with you. Instead, whoever wants to become great among you must be your servant, and whoever wants to be first must be your slave – just as the Son of Man did not come to be served, but to serve...*
> [Matthew 20:25-28]

Service is a matter of the heart. I've seen women serve, and all the while, sensed the anger and the contempt burning in them. They're not fooling anyone, not even themselves. A person motivated by outside pressures, or fear, is not ministering. Service is the expression of servanthood, and servanthood is the expression of love. The greatest role in God's kingdom is servant. [Matthew 23:11]

No one in God's kingdom is able to "fake it 'til you

make it." For a season, someone may put on a show or an act. Giftings and talents can carry a person for a while. However, charlatans always get exposed. Unless there are strong internal motivators, ministry fizzles. The greatest motivator is love. When a woman loves someone, and therefore serves, she is able to deny her needs for the needs of others. Personal denial is difficult even when motivated by love, nevertheless, the joy and the pleasure overshadow the cost. Love won't give up.

Years ago, I had gallstones. The first attack occurred late one evening. I got out of bed, and vomited. The pain was so intense I curled up in the fetal position on the floor. My ex-wife said she was tired, and wanted to sleep. The pain intensified. While on the floor, with a bed pan in front of me, I called the information nurse at the hospital. She advised me to get to the hospital a.s.a.p. Once again, my wife slept. I drove myself to the hospital. The nurse gave me two shots of Demerol before the pain was bearable.

Flash forward seven years. I battled kidney stones this time. While I attended a house gathering in the mountains, an attack struck. I ate pain pills, and a friend drove me off the mountain to my car. The twenty-four hour flu bug made the rounds too. By the time I reached my car, I ran a temperature, and vomited. My friend followed me home. My grandmother and I lived together. At home, I vomited, had diarrhea, and couldn't urinate. Throughout the night, my ninety year old grandmother changed my bed pan, and rubbed my feet. I've seen Jesus and he lives in the heart of my grandmother.

My grandmother is among the greatest servants. Throughout her entire life, she has ministered to hurting family and friends. Even animals received God's love through her. Women who walk in true servanthood possess a grace that men will never possess. To truly serve, one must truly love. Scripture also says,

> *Do nothing out of selfish ambition or vain conceit, but in humility consider others better than yourselves. Each of you should look not only to your own interests, but also to the interests of others. Your attitude should be the same as that of Christ Jesus.* [Philippians 2:3-5]

When Jesus was arrested and crucified, the inner twelve deserted him. Yet, the women who ministered to Jesus stayed with him through the crucifixion and resurrection. [Matthew 27:55-56, 28:1-10] They served their Lord and Savior in life and death.

The role of women in ministry is controversial. I think if a person is honest with themselves, the issue is mute. If one surveys the scriptures, women function in the same ministry roles as do men; leader, intercessor, prophet, apostle, pastor, evangelist, teacher, and worker of miracles etc. Consider experience too. From what I witnessed, women possess all the same giftings. In the New Testament, the ministry role women appear to be excluded from is elder or overseer. I'm unable to find a single example. Furthermore, a woman functioning as an elder contradicts the prescriptive order found elsewhere in the bible.

As men are to the family, so elders are to the local body; *Elders direct the affairs of the church.* [1Timothy 5:17] Elders are the fathers of the house. In Acts, a decision was made regarding the "gentile controversy" by the apostles and elders with the support of the entire Jerusalem church. [Acts 15:22] The letter sent with Paul and Barnabas was addressed as, "*The apostles and elders, your brothers.*" [Acts 15:23] Oversight is about guidance. In decision making, the final word is reserved for the fathers of the family, and for the fathers of God's family.

This train of thought leads to another difficult issue, "yokes." Say for example God joined a man and a woman together as husband and wife. In many circumstances, home and ministry are divided. A wife submits to her husband at home. In ministry, however, a husband may be required to submit to his wife because of her title and position in a pyramided church structure. These types of arrangements put husbands and wives in precarious situations. Husbands gradually withdraw, and avoid spiritual functions altogether. In turn, wives assert their church titles and positions at home, and eventually end-up providing spiritual leadership for their families. A wife who dominates the spiritual climate, and provides guidance for the household, "wears the pants in the family." Sadly, these arrangements are more normative than exceptional. God's order is perverted. A wife's primary responsibility is to God, and secondly to her husband. Ministry is third. The order for husbands is the same; God, wife, ministry.

The only context which allows husbands and wives to fully express and use their ministry roles and functions together are small intimate settings. Here, if a spouse is spiritually inept, he or she can quickly grow and mature. Couples function in complimentary relationships, rather than ones of domination and superiority. In a short time, husband and wife are ministering as a couple.

In Genesis 1:27 it says,

> *So God created man in his own image, in the image of God he created him; male and female he created them.*

From this passage, female is as much the image of God, as is male. And verse 28 says,

> *God blessed them and said to them, Be fruitful and increase in number; fill the earth and subdue it. Rule over the fish of the sea and the birds of the air and over every living creature that moves on the ground.*

Authority is a benchmark of a godly woman. Scripture is clear that men and women were designed to co-rule and subdue together. Women are called to exercise authority over the elements, sickness and disease, and dark powers. Within western culture, godly women have exercised more spiritual authority than Christian men. The church rules and reigns with the Lord Jesus Christ. The body of Christ exercises the same authority and dominion as He does. Scripture says,

> *That power is like the working of his mighty strength, which he exerted in Christ when he raised him from the dead and seated him at his right hand in the heavenly realms, far above all rule and authority, power and dominion, and every title that can be given, not only in the present age but also in the one to come. And God placed all things under his feet and appointed him to be head over everything for the church, which is his body, the fullness of him who fills everything in every way.* [Ephesians 1:19-23]

When a woman knows Jesus as her Lord and Savior, and therefore, she is a part of the church, she has authority. Even before the church age, and the atoning work of Jesus Christ, it says,

> "*Women of faith received back their dead,*

raised to life again." [Hebrews 11:35]

That's power. That's authority.

1 Timothy 2:15 says,

> *But women will be saved through childbearing – if they continue in faith, love and holiness with propriety.*

For many believers this passage seems strange and difficult to understand. Others look for a deep, dark mysterious meaning. However, if once again, the whole of scripture is considered, the passage is simple and straightforward. In the garden, Eve ate the forbidden fruit. By doing so, she presumptuously usurped Adam as the man and head of their relationship. God made the punishment fit the transgression. The bible says,

> "...Y*our desire will be for your husband, and he will rule over you.*" [Genesis 3:16]

Here, *desire* has nothing to do with sexuality. It doesn't fit the context. God's declaration of punishment could be rephrased, "You will want the role of your husband, but he is going to lord over you." Unfulfilled desires foster frustration and friction, and sometimes animosity.

Paul hammers, over and over again, for women to submit. Submission is the door out of the "Fall" induced punishment. Men were never intended to dominate women. Nowhere in scripture does God tell men, or women for that matter, to rule over the other. Domination and superiority is the result of the Fall and sin.

In the 1Timothy passage Paul exhorts women to stay within their role. Men will never birth babies. Birthing is the glorious role exclusively of women. If a woman attempts to take the role of man, once again, she becomes frustrated and bitter. Everywhere I go, I run into hateful, angry women. Many of these gals are divorced, by themselves, and raising children. In virtually every city, there are churches who practice what they preach, and provide needed assistance to single, struggling mothers. Find one -- they're out there.

Very, very few people are called to be single. Even if a woman is divorced, the Lord may intend for her to remarry. Is divorce and remarriage the ideal situation? Hardly. The Lord hates divorce. [Malachi 2:16] Some circumstances may lie outside of one's control too; abuse, adultery, or even the other spouse choosing and petitioning for divorce.

Western believers are very selective where they extend grace. I've never understood how Christians feel they can pick and choose which sins are forgivable, and which sins aren't. Scripture is quite clear,

> *For whoever keeps the whole law and yet stumbles at just one point is guilty of breaking all of it.* [James 2:10]

We are all just as guilty as any divorcee, murderer or thief. Moreover, even God's been divorced. [Jeremiah 3:8]

Women, and men for that matter, are prone to remarrying the same kind of person all over again. I did. People gravitate towards the familiar, good and bad alike. Women need to start with godliness and friendship. Bank accounts cannot buy happiness. A few women are called gold-diggers for a reason. There are no guarantees in life, but, by beginning with godly values, the odds are life will go much better.

If we need fathers, we also need mothers. Children are commanded by God to honor their mother like their father. [Exodus 20:12] Only a woman can fulfill the role of mother; birthing and nurturing children. Men participate in nurturing too, but, women are specifically designed for the caring process.

Mothers received special revelation regarding the destiny of their children which was not always shared with the fathers. Rebekah knew from birth the destinies of Jacob and Esau. [Genesis 25:23] Moses' mother recognized the calling on him. [Exodus 2:1-10] Mary was foretold the life of her son, Jesus. [Luke 1:30-33]

If nature is important, nurture is equally important. Environmental factors ignite blessings or curses which are passed down genetically. A godly wife and mother will create a healthy ambience or atmosphere in a household. Godliness retards curses and ignites blessings.

Jacob, while tending flocks for his father-in-law Laban, separated the dark and spotted animals for himself. [Genesis 30:32] Later, he carved up tree limbs, exposing white and dark areas, and planted them in the watering holes of his livestock. [Genesis 30:37-38] When the animals mated, they saw speckled limbs, and in turn, produced speckled offspring. Jacob's flock greatly increased. [Genesis 30:43] By altering the environment, Jacob changed the genetics of his animals.

Mothers determine their family environment too. I've witnessed this in my own family. My mother stayed home and cared for her family. We all received educations, but most importantly, we all serve the Lord. I remember as a little boy, my mother asked if I wanted to be baptized in the Holy Spirit. I did, and she prayed with me, my father, and my siblings. Our entire family was baptized in the Spirit. I lived in a godly household. She is now helping to raise her grandchildren. My mother has blessed generations.

Women are predisposed toward certain sins as well. Some gals are called "gold-diggers," while others are accused of pursuing a "sugar-daddy." All women search for security. Money translates into security, doesn't it: a good provider, a bigger home, a nicer neighborhood, a luxury sedan, a cruise, and so on? Money changes structures and conditions, yet fails to deliver peace of mind and contentment of heart. Wealthy socialites check into rehabs because money could not satisfy their innate desires. Many of these troubled women are in their late teens or early twenties.

Women compromise values and convictions for fear of being abandoned and having to fend for themselves and their children. Females have a greater propensity for fear than do males. As men attempt to satiate their God-given desire for companionship with sex, so women attempt to satiate their God-given desire for security with money.

Security is a simplistic answer. The core or real answer lies much deeper. The vast majority of women, like men, were never meant to be alone. If woman was created for man, then it stands to reason, a satisfaction or need is met for women by being in a proper relationship with men. Men and women "fit" together.

I've heard women say, "Jesus is my covering" or "Jesus is my head." Statements like these come out rejection and bitterness. If God called a woman to celibacy, she should walk in that grace. However, like men, celibacy is the exception, not the norm. Yes, ultimately Jesus is the head over all. Somehow though, many Christians believe with the coming of Christ, everything prior is null and void. I know Christians who never read the Old Testament. A few believers only own a New Testament. Yet, God's design never changed. As it was in the beginning, so it will be in the end. Jesus restores, and enables believers to reenter the Garden experience. God's purposes and plans are the same today as they were in the beginning.

For a woman to realize her complete feminine nature, she needs a proper relationship with a man. Manhood draws forth womanhood, and womanhood draws forth manhood. Pseudo-security like money, or a God-compromising relationship cannot provide any lasting peace or satisfaction.

In 1Timothy 5, Paul counsels Timothy on church affairs. Women, in particular, struggle with gossip. Paul states,

> *Besides, they get into the habit of being idle and going about from house to house. And not only do they become idlers, but also gossips and busybodies, saying things they ought not to. So I counsel younger widows to marry, to have children, to manage their homes and to give the enemy no opportunity for slander.* [1Timothy 5:13-14]

A house church leader by the name of John Fenn spoke on John 10:10 which reads,

> *The thief comes only to steal and kill and destroy; I have come that they may have life, and have it to the full.*

Originally, I took this scripture at face value; Satan ruins people, and Jesus brings life. Mr. Fenn, however, brought fresh understanding. [Fenn] As the Lord has saints working for righteousness, so Satan has workers of iniquity. Satan uses people to steal, kill, and destroy. How? People gossip about, and slander others. First, a person's honor and reputation is stolen through gossip. This is character assassination. After an assassination, a person's relationships shrivel up and die. People are social creatures, and without meaningful relationships, a person becomes isolated, and is eventually destroyed.

Before I was even divorced, my ex-wives phoned

friends and family, and told them how "evil" I was. I was a godparent to several children, and I never heard from any of those people again. Although women have a greater propensity to gossip, men also fall prey to this terrible habit. Some men within the church are full-blown assassins. Like everyone else, I'm also guilty. People are responsible for what they know. Now, you know. Stop gossiping women. Confess your sin to God, and others if need be, and go forward.

Another pitfall for women is their use of manipulation to get control. If every man's disease is lust, every woman's disease is control and manipulation. I have never met a woman who has not struggled in these areas. The diabolical two are rooted in the fallen feminine nature. Remember,

> "*Your desire will be for your husband, and he will rule over you.*" [Genesis 3:16]

Women are not going too physically overpower men. In their fallen nature, women use control and manipulation while attempting to attain a position of dominance over men, and other women. Men struggle with control and manipulation too, just as women can struggle with lust.

Control and manipulation are weapons of choice for women. For this reason, the spirit of Jezebel gravitates towards femininity. Ahab and Jezebel were the epitome of a fallen, perverted relationship. [1 Kings 16:31] An Ahab/Jezebel relationship is one which completely contradicts God's order; "Ahabs" abdicate headship, while "Jezebels" rule through control and manipulation. A while back, a good friend informed me that a prominent Christian speaker stated she saw the spirit of Jezebel working more through men than women in the church. Why is that? Please recall what I said earlier, "There is a lack of manliness in the body of Christ." Too many men in the church are overtly feminine. Jezebel, a satanic power, is once again, predisposed to femininity.

Jezebel is the archenemy of the prophets. Prophets bring proper order; men being men and women being women. Jezebel usurps, distorts and turns God's order upside down. Behind control and manipulation is fear. When a person is fearful, they use whatever means necessary for protection and preservation, and to achieve their desired ends. The antidote of course is love. When believers are secure in the Lord, they trust Him to work all things for their good. [Romans 8:28] Sometimes, moments or snapshots in our lives seem unfair, and they very well may be, but, if we are faithful and do as the Lord commands us through scripture, He will work everything out on our behalf. Humility and submission are the literal antitheses to control and manipulation. Paul said,

> *"...So also wives should submit to their husbands in everything."* [Ephesians 5:22]

I hope you're not feeling overwhelmed. Perhaps you're thinking, "My life is a mess." To be quite frank, your life may be a mess. However, don't give up.

Some years ago, I took Thai kickboxing. On one occasion, my instructor said something very interesting, "A fight is never won with one punch." Sometimes, believers want the battle over with one new revelation, or one victory. Life doesn't work that way.

Keep punching. Win the war, and not just the battle. God is with you. You're overcoming.

THE CHURCH

Poor man wanna be rich
Rich man wanna be king
And the king ain't satisfied 'til he rules everything
BRUCE SPRINGSTEEN *BADLANDS*

While living in Montana, I exercised at a little independently owned, hard-core gym. The owner made his own equipment and machines. I saw an Olympic weight-lifting set there too. I asked him who used the set, and he said he did. He proceeded to tell me his story.

Originally, he was a body builder. Body builders sculpt and shape their bodies by focusing on certain muscle groups. Eventually he became bored, and started power lifting. Power lifters bulk up, and attempt to lift as much weight as they can in three events; bench press, dead lift, and squats. Once again though, dissatisfaction set in. He then turned to Olympic lifting. Here, a lifter picks weight up from the floor, and attempts to raise the bar above his head. There are two events in Olympic lifting; cling and jerk, and snatch. The owner told me he would never go back to the other forms of lifting.

I had a similar encounter while traveling in the southern part of the state. I met a woman who was an avid hunter. She started hunting with a rifle. After she became successful with a rifle, she tried black powder. It proved to be a greater challenge, and she enjoyed hunting even more. She then began bow hunting. The bow was her favorite. She, like the weight lifter, said she would never go back.

The human spirit has an innate drive or quest to find the essence or the heart of the matter. If a person stays with an activity long enough, they'll sever the frills and the gimmicks, routine becomes a passion, and eventually, their efforts become a personalized creative expression. Purists want the raw and the simple, the primitive.

Years ago, Robert Pirsig wrote the now classic *Zen and The Art of Motorcycle Maintenance*. [Pirsig] He tells the story of how he and his son rode around the country on a small 250cc motorcycle. Soon, the care of his motorcycle was no longer cause and effect, or just mechanical. Rather, the bike was seemingly alive. Pirsig treated his motorcycle like a living entity; he understood the bike's needs, limitations and strengths. He customized parts, surpassing the manufacturer's specifications. Within every field, whether it's sports, technology, or cooking, there are a few purists who passionately pursue new territory.

Most people though, are defined by peers and contemporaries. Like sheep, people feel safest surrounded by others. Mediocrity is simply accepting and complying with the values of the larger group. Fear keeps people from transgressing the expected norm. Eventually, a person is indistinguishable from everyone else.

I once asked a woman what she wanted out of life, and her response was, "I want a house with a white picket fence." I queried, "You want mediocrity?" She said, "That's exactly what I want." Unless dissatisfaction arises in a person, or something jars them loose, they settle for the norm, or mediocrity.

The American church became increasingly complex and ornate. Services are well-rehearsed productions. The basic structure of the church has not changed for hundreds of years. What many believers consider sacred never existed until the church married paganism in the fourth century.

I also encounter many church-goers who parrot the latest fad or doctrine proclaimed from the pulpit. Many teachings simply spin cultural ideologies which resonate with our wicked hearts, and we cling to them like our favorite teddy bear. Few believers ask themselves, "Why?"

The modern sanctuary appeals to the modern consumer: gold pillars, posh carpet, comfortable chairs, cappuccino bars, flat screens, glass podiums, Italian tiled restrooms, and rock star sound systems. The argument is, "God deserves the best." Why was Jesus born in a manger and not a palace? [Luke 2:7] Why did the early believers meet in homes? [Acts 20:20, Romans 16:5] Believers, like everyone else, lie to themselves. God does not need our stuff. Scripture is very clear,

> *"What is highly valued among men is detestable in God's sight."* [Luke 16:15]

> Paul says in 1 Corinthians 9:19-22,

> *Though I am free and belong to no man, I make myself a slave to everyone, to win as many as possible. To the Jews I became like a Jew, to win the Jews. To those under the law I became as like one under the law (though myself am not under the law), so as to win those under the law. To those not having the law I became like one not having the law (though I am not free from God's law but am under Christ's law), so as to win those not having the law. To the weak I became weak, to win the weak. I have*

> *become all things to all men so that by all possible means I might save some.*

Christian leaders interpret this passage to imply cultural relevancy and sensitivity, and use it to launch ministries. Their churches rival the local sports bar for entertainment or the local skate park for fun. Other churches emphasize comfort and prosperity in order to draw the community's elite. Is this wrong? No. Scripture says,

> *The important thing is that in every way, whether from false motives or true, Christ is preached.* [Philippians 1:18]

However, believers fail to grasp the deeper meaning of the Corinthians passage. Even Peter said of Paul,

> *His letters contain some things that are hard to understand, which ignorant and unstable people distort, as they do the others scriptures, to their own destruction.* [2 Peter 3:16]

What is 1 Corinthians 9:19-22 saying then? Was Paul the consummate chameleon? With Jews, he acted like a Jew, and with the unlawful, he broke the law? Hardly! Rather, Paul was saying he accepted others for who they were, regardless of their place or position in life.

Jesus, who is the model for all of Christian life, always accepted others. Nevertheless, he did not become a prostitute to reach the prostitutes. [Matthew 9:10-13] I've seen many brothers and sisters in Christ confuse the 1 Corinthians passage, and soon, they dress and act like someone they're not. Whether rich or poor, black or white, male or female, most people eventually recognize the posers from the genuine. Jesus was like his heavenly

Father, as was Paul.

Churches have sought people instead of the glory of God. American culture tells us, "Newer and bigger is better." Success is based on numbers (people) and tithes (money). Believers also resort to Christian magic. In other words, if believers know the formula or the technique, then they can build a big ministry too. Ministers trot the globe attending seminars and conferences hoping to discover the secret formula. Others want an impartation. They pursue anointed prophets and apostles like rock star groupies.

The vast majority of believers are quite comfortable with the present church structure. Traditional church is safe, and requires little or no effort. For years on end, a person can sit in the same spot Sunday after Sunday, listen to sermon after sermon, and never change. Traditional church is structurally unsound, and therefore, often inhibits the transformation of believers. However, believers and nonbelievers alike are creatures of habit. Few believers step out, and try something different. They're just too comfortable.

A train of thought in physics goes like this: An existing order gets nudged, temporarily becoming disorderly. The disorder potentially leads to a greater order than existed prior to the nudge. Likewise, believers often associate misfortune or seeming failure with the work of the devil. Yet, God allows perceived misfortune to dislodge believers from feeble, broken conditions. He acts on behalf of believers everywhere to bring greater understanding and order to their lives.

A few believers are on a quest. They seek their faith's most essential form and structure. Others get nudged by the Holy Spirit, and know something's terribly wrong. And still others have experienced hardship and tragedy, and found themselves needing more. God's in the whole process. He looked on the hearts of these believers, and has strategically orchestrated circumstances to keep them moving forward on the path of life. They're in store for the richest season of their lives.

We have been moving in concentric circles: the inner circle is the individual heart; next is men and women; and the outer circle is the church. This defines a radical restructuring of life. Believers position themselves for the glory of God when there is proper order. Where God is, there is life.

The church is portrayed as a beautiful bride in the book of Ephesians. [vs 5:25-33] It is also seen as the body of Christ. [Ephesians 4:12] Another definition is when two or more believers gather in the name of Jesus. [Matthew 18:20] Within our modern culture, church is a physical building. Each depiction carries a reality. However, none of the images are all encompassing. The church is mysterious.

The areas of life which are extremely intimate, are by far the most difficult to understand. Jesus said,

> *Why do you look at the speck of sawdust in your brother's eye and pay no attention to the plank in your own eye?* [Luke 6:41]

We easily see the faults in others, but to see ourselves, as we are, requires the illumination of the Holy Spirit.

I remember Easter egg hunting as a child. I always found the egg stuffed in a hole or in the bushes. In fact, the more obscure the place, the harder I looked. However, an egg that sat on a table, or on a ledge or in plain view, I overlooked; those eggs were too close to me. The church is like that. Believers are the church. Since the church is so intimate, so close to the believer, it becomes very difficult to see and identify.

God's intentions never changed. Outright rebellion

from fallen angels or mankind is not going to circumvent or deter His plans. God is God. If believers are going to understand God's earliest intention, they have to investigate beginnings or firsts.

A number of believers would start with Acts 2 and the day of Pentecost, or the "birth" of the church. Yet, the birth of the church was simply a restoration of God's primary purpose. Genesis reveals His plan. God's first engagement with man was creating man. Scripture says,

> *...the Lord formed the man from the dust of the ground and breathed into his nostrils the breath of life, and the man became a living being.* [Genesis 2:7]

Man did not live until God breathed in him. Life came from the Spirit of God. Here is a truth; as blood is to flesh, so the Spirit of God is to the church. Without blood, flesh eventually dies. Blood carries biological DNA determining who and what we are as humans. Without the Spirit, there is no church. God's people are established by God's DNA, or Spirit. Each person who possesses the Spirit of God is a member of the church. Romans 8:9 says,

> "*...And if anyone does not have the Spirit of Christ, he does not belong to Christ.*"

If a person does not belong to Christ, they do not belong to the church. With the gift of the Holy Spirit, believers are progressively transformed into the image and likeness of Christ. Scripture also says,

> *For those God foreknew he also predestined to be conformed to the likeness*

> *of his Son, that he might be the firstborn among many brothers.* [Romans 8:29]

Since Spirit supersedes soul and flesh, one's entire being should be altered, including their mind and body. God flows through believers! They are the children of God.

We are given a prophetic picture of the church in John 2:1-11. The bible says,

> *On the third day a wedding took place at Cana in Galilee. Jesus' mother was there and Jesus and his disciples had also been invited to the wedding. When the wine was gone, Jesus' mother said to him, They have no more wine. Dear woman, why do you involve me? Jesus replied. My time has not yet come. His mother said to the servants, Do whatever he tells you. Nearby stood six stone water jars, the kind used by the Jews for ceremonial washing, each holding from twenty to thirty gallons. Jesus said to the servants, Fill the jars with water; so they filled them to the brim. Then he told them, Now draw some out and take it to the master of the banquet. They did so, and the master of the banquet tasted the water that had been turned into wine. He did not realize where it had come from, though the servants who had drawn the water knew. Then he called the bridegroom aside and said, Everyone brings out the choice wine first and then the cheaper wine after the guests have had too much to drink; but you have saved the best till now.*

The miracle occurred on the third day of the wedding. Three is symbolic of the Godhead and triune man, but also represents resurrection power. [John 2:19-22] Power is simply the ability to bring about change. Jesus changed water into wine. The human body is approximately two-thirds water. Wine is eighty-five to ninety percent water. To take water and turn it into wine a transformation must take place. Likewise, the church is transformed from the natural or human, into the supernatural body of Christ through resurrection power. [Ephesians 4:12] Believers, as the church, are the new wine. Six stone water jars were used. Six is the number of man. God created man on the sixth day. [Genesis 1:24-31] Furthermore, those jars were used for ceremonial washing. Water symbolizes the word of God. [Ephesians 5:26] As vessels of God, believers cleanse those around them through preaching and teaching of the word of God. Those six jars held from twenty to thirty gallons. Twenty is the number of expectancy. For example, Israel waited twenty years for deliverance from the Philistines through Samson. [Judges 15:20] Thirty is the number of readiness or maturity. Jesus was thirty years old when he began his ministry. [Luke 3:23] And Joseph, a type of Jesus, began his rule at thirty. [Genesis 41:46] Isn't this just like the church? Some believers continue to wait, expectantly, to step into their destinies. Others are there, ready and walking in those things God purposed for them. Even Jesus made the claim, "*My time has not yet come.*"

I want you to know, the world has been waiting for you. You have something that only you can bring to others. Many times, just like Jesus, we feel our time has yet to come. However, the Lord places us in situations which pulls our destinies into being. Difficult situations take us from expectancy to maturity.

The wedding where the miracle of the wine happened took place in Cana. Cana means zealous or acquired. [Jackson 21] There are people in your office, at school, or maybe even family members, who are crying out in their hearts. Those who sought Jesus were always blessed. At present, he is seated at the right hand of the Father. [Ephesians 1:20] Jesus is pouring out his new wine, us, to all who would drink. This is why scripture says,

> *The creation waits in eager expectation for the sons of God to be revealed. For the creation was subjected to frustration, not by its own choice, but by the will of the one who subjected it, in hope that the creation itself will be liberated from its bondage to decay and brought into the glorious freedom of the children of God.*
> [Romans 8:19-21]

As the sons of God are revealed, they intoxicate the world.

Some believers contend, "God is the new wine poured into us, the new wineskin." To be sure, God does pour Himself into believers. [Acts 2:4] However, believers must be more expansive in their understanding of scriptures. Their thinking sometimes becomes rigid and prevents them from moving into new insights. God said to Moses, "*I Am Who I am.*" [Exodus 3:14] He also said, "*I the Lord do not change.*" [Malachi 3:6]

God is not in process, or becoming as in Hegelian philosophy. He is not new. God is who He is. What He reveals to believers, the church, may be new and often is. With each generation, God seemingly reveals more of Himself, as believers become able to receive greater understanding. If He revealed the fullness of His glory, all at once, we would be destroyed. God meets the church where they're at, and what they can handle.

I've also heard this, "God is doing things not found in scripture." My response is, "Yes He is." I'm very open to extra-biblical revelation and manifestations, and so should every believer, as long as God is glorified. In Mark 16:17 and 20 it says,

> *"And these signs will accompany those who believe..."*

And,

> *Then the disciples went out and preached everywhere, and the Lord worked with them and confirmed his word by the signs that accompanied it.*

God blesses people, and loves them, even those who do not worship Him. He is a good God. He does things that draw people to Him. Since the word of God reveals who God is, He proves His word through tangible expressions of His glory, or signs and wonders. A sign indicates or directs.

For example, if I'm on a road and a sign says, "Seattle 15 miles," and I'm traveling to Seattle, I know I'm on the right road. If the sign said, "New York 15 miles," and again, I'm going to Seattle, I'm way off course. A God-sign directs people to God, or draws attention to Him. If the miraculous draws attention to someone or something else, beware. Signs and wonders indicate authorship.

Sometimes believers elevate God's workers to a position and a stature they have no business occupying in their lives. Paul said,

> *...One of you says, I follow Paul, another, I follow Apollos, another I follow Cephas; still another, I follow Christ. Is Christ divided? Was Paul crucified for you? Were you baptized into the name of Paul?*
>
> [1 Corinthians 1:12-13]

There were groupies in Paul's day, and there are groupies today. Believers become mesmerized with a gifting or ministry which is simply a conduit for the love of God. Again, believers must seek the Author, and not the vessel.

Groupies are only the tip of the iceberg though. Immaturity is pervasive throughout the American church. I also hear phrases like, "We need to be more like little children." Here, the thinking is if believers view themselves as children, and God is their Daddy, they somehow become godlier.

Years ago, I worked for a company which had a biweekly ritual. When someone received a check, whether for five dollars or a thousand, everyone else was expected to cheer for them as they ran forward to collect their money. The leader's explanation was, "People who think cheering is silly have never won anything in their lives. They don't know what it feels like." The opposite is true. I watched Jerry Rice play football. He scored so many times, that after a touchdown, he calmly dropped the ball, or tossed it to a referee, and jogged to the sidelines. Other players danced, rolled around, or performed a little show. They rarely scored.

For many believers, crawling up into Daddy's lap is a new experience. The church is filled with orphans. God is a Daddy or Poppy to all of us. If this is what someone needs, and every believer does at times, God will meet them at their need. However, God does not want His church to be perpetually infantile. Once again, scripture is construed. The bible says,

> *At that time the disciples came to Jesus and asked, Who is the greatest in the kingdom of heaven? He called a little child and had him stand among them. And he said: I tell*

> *you the truth, unless you change and become like little children, you will never enter the kingdom of heaven. Therefore, whoever humbles himself like this child is the greatest in the kingdom of heaven.* [Matthew 18:1-4]

Children are unpretentious and easily believe. This is what scripture means to be "childlike." Believers must get over themselves, and stop being so concerned what others think. One of the greatest sins is unbelief. As sons and daughters of God, the church is called to believe their heavenly Father. Scripture says,

> *God is not a man, that he should lie, nor a son of man, that he should change his mind.* [Numbers 23:19]

If a person wants to work for God, or serve, here's what they do, believe! 1 John 3:23-24 says,

> *And this is his command: to believe in the name of his Son, Jesus Christ, and to love one another as he commanded us. Those who obey his commands live in him, and he in them. And this is how we know he lives in us: We know it by the Spirit he gave us.*

Belief precedes action and obedience. Why do little children set cookies and milk out by the Christmas tree? Children believe in Santa Claus. Since children really believe, they act on those beliefs. When Christians really believe in Jesus, the Son of God, they obey the bible. Working for God is simply believing God.

1 Corinthians 13:13 says,

> "*And now these three remain: faith, hope, and love. But the greatest of these is love.*"

Love anchors faith and hope. Without love, faith and hope will gradually lose power and strength. God demonstrates His love to each believer in unique, tender ways. That love is kindled and matures. Believers learn to trust God. Through each season, their faith grows. Believers eventually say, "Yes and Amen!" to the bizarre things God whispers in their ears, and the strange stories read in the bible.

Wholehearted, unreserved belief is maturity. The kingdom of heaven contradicts the kingdoms of this world: the Lord is born in a manger, and has no home; princes are desert dwelling prophets; by losing your life, you find it; the last is really first; giving is receiving; a coward defeats an army; a prostitute saves her family; fishermen speak before rulers and powerful authorities; and childlike faith is maturity. God is not interested in a heavenly day care. Jesus is not pursuing a little girl. Rather, he is patiently waiting for his young, beautiful bride to mature, and co-rule with him throughout eternity. Scripture says,

> *Let us rejoice and be glad and give him glory! For the wedding of the Lamb has come, and his bride has made herself ready. Fine linen, bright and clean, was given her to wear. (*Fine linen stands for the righteous acts of the saints) [Revelation 19:7]

Righteous acts flow out of a believing heart. The bible also says,

> *...Until we all reach unity in the faith and in the knowledge of the Son of God and become mature, attaining to the whole*

> *measure of the fullness of Christ. Then we will no longer be infants...* [Ephesians 4:13-14]

Many believers cry out for heavenly experiences, and revelation. They've heard someone on a tape, or at a conference, share a heavenly encounter. A believer then says to themselves, "I sure wish that was me" or "Why can't I have that experience?" God honors extended prayer and fasting. Yet, where is the line; a day, a month, three months? Heavenly experiences begin with faith or believing. If Peter and Paul had heavenly visitations, so can others. Believe! Scripture is clear, "*For God does not show favoritism.*" [Romans 2:11]

Believers can never make themselves holy enough though. Many Christians work or strive for God's attention like love-starved orphans. Tantrums won't turn His head either. Jesus said,

> "*Blessed are the pure in heart, for they will see God.*" [Matthew 5:8]

Believers do not purify their hearts and then see God. Rather, they encounter God, and then their hearts are purified. Then, and only then, does the believer see with spiritual eyes.

Isaiah cried out,

> *I am ruined! For I am a man of unclean lips, and I live among a people of unclean lips, and my eyes have seen the King, the Lord Almighty.* [Isaiah 6:5]

In other words, Isaiah had a dirty mouth because of an impure heart. What purified him?

> *Then one of the seraphs flew to me with a live coal in his hand, which he had taken with tongs from the alter. With it he touched my mouth and said, See, this has touched your lips: your guilt is taken away and your sin atoned for.* [Isaiah 6:6-7]

A God-encounter purified Isaiah, enabling him to see hundreds of years into the future. God purifies believers. Now, this does not mean believers passively stare at the sky hoping some angel will fall out of the clouds and change them. Position yourself.

God says,

> *Ask and it will be given to you; seek and you will find; knock and the door will be opened to you. For everyone who asks receives; he who seeks finds; and to him who knocks, the door will be opened. Which of you, if his son asks for bread, will be given a stone? Or if he asks for a fish, will give him a snake? If you, then, though you are evil, know how to give good gifts to your children how much more will your Father in heaven give good gifts to those who ask him!* [Matthew 7:7-11]

If you desire to know the mysteries of God, ask Him. If you want to see God, seek Him. If you want to know what heaven is like, knock on His heart. And when you ask, seek, or knock… believe! He is a good God. So often, God immediately responds, and believers dismiss a thought as wild imagination, or a dream as too much pizza, or a strange encounter as coincidence. God is not a chatterbox, but He constantly speaks to His children.

Recently, my wife and I looked for an apartment.

We also looked at property on Thirteenth Street for a new business. Property on this street is outrageously priced. A little discouraged, I went to a theatre to watch a movie. My movie played in the thirteenth theater of twenty-one cinemas. God? Sure, He's always speaking.

Next, we saw nice apartments on Thirteenth Street. I received a word God was moving us up. The apartment complex on Thirteenth Street just happened to have an opening. The flat was $250 cheaper than the other apartments we saw, and nicer. Our last apartment was 407, and this one was 408; we were moving up. Also, these apartments were only five minutes from my wife's work. Everything fit. God spoke loud and clear.

Most believers know the story of Jesus walking on water; in the story Peter attempts walking out to Him. [Matthew 14:22-33] I've heard countless sermons on how Peter took his eyes off Jesus, and sank. [Matthew 14:30] Conversely, I've heard numerous sermons praising Peter for getting out of the boat, and trying. [Matthew 14:29] Yet, I'm convinced both interpretations are superficial renderings. Why did Jesus walk on water? Was it in order to show off or demonstrate his power? Why did He call Peter to himself? Because Peter asked? When Peter sank, Jesus caught him and said, "*You of little faith... why did you doubt*?" [Matthew 14:31]

Here again is the theme of faith or believing. Jesus said,

> *I tell you the truth, if you have faith as small as a mustard seed, you can say to this mountain, Move from here to there and it*
>
> *will move. Nothing will be impossible for you.* [Matthew 17:20-21]

Believing is an important key to the kingdom of God.

Jesus walked on water to demonstrate the principles of his kingdom. He taught his disciples how his world functions. With the miracle of feeding the five thousand, Jesus explicitly challenged His disciples, "*You give them something to eat.*" [Matthew 9:13]

Jesus was training His disciples, as well as us, to be children of God. His realm completely supersedes the natural world. Jesus sent the twelve disciples out doing kingdom work of healing the sick and casting out demons. [Mark 9:12-13]

I recently read *Parallel Worlds* by Michio Kaku. Kaku is a world class physicist and cofounder of string-field theory. Physicists know we live in three dimensions of space [length, width, and breadth] and with time an added fourth dimension. Some thinkers theorize there could be as many as eleven dimensions. Kaku points out that a being existing in the fifth dimension would not be confined by the same natural laws and principles as someone who is constrained to four dimensions. [Kaku 199, 219-221] Expressed another way, a being from the fifth dimension would have abilities that humans don't possess. Jesus is the Lord of the fifth dimension and all other dimensions. He said,

> "*I am the way and the truth and the life.*"
> [John 14:6]

If believing is an important key to the kingdom of God, then Jesus is the only door people can enter through. It is His domain.

At the beginning of his earthly ministry Jesus said, "*Repent for the kingdom of heaven is near.*" [Matthew 4:17] After his death and resurrection, people could enter in, and live life as it was originally intended by our Creator. Jesus showed the way to the Father. The very nature of truth is exclusive. Jesus is the truth; He is the only means of entering the kingdom of God. He is the life; in Him, believers can live in other dimensions, even now.

At the end of the Gospel of John it says,

> *But these are written that you may believe that Jesus is the Christ, the Son of God, and that by believing you may have life in his name.* [John 20:31]

This means the limitations of a fallen, broken world are destroyed through the power of the gospel of the Lord Jesus Christ. The life of each and every believer is supposed to be extraordinary, even superhuman, like Jesus.

The temple of God was considered the habitation of God. [1 Kings 8:10] God lived in the temple. Yet, the Old Testament temple was a shadowy image of things to come, alluding to a new habitation. With the atoning sacrifice of Jesus Christ, believers became God's dwelling place. It says in Hebrews 10:10 and verse 14,

> *And by that will, we have been made holy through the sacrifice of the body of Jesus Christ once and for all... because by one sacrifice he has made perfect forever those who are being made holy.*

Believers are the new habitation of God. Paul says in 1Corinthians 3:16,

> *Don't you know that you yourselves are God's temple and that God's Spirit lives in you? If anyone destroys God's temple; God will destroy him; for God's temple is sacred, and you are that temple.*

Even Jesus said,

> *...The kingdom of God does not come with your careful observation, will people say, Here it is, or There it is, because the kingdom of God is within you.* [Luke 17:20-21]

There is no kingdom without a king. And where the king rules, the kingdom is established. Jesus is the King of kings. Just as those earthen vessels were filled with water, and transformed into wine, believers, as earthen vessels, filled with the Spirit, are transformed into heavenly beings. God's children are glory carriers. His presence was so strong in Peter that even his shadow healed people. [Acts 5:15] Note again, 2 Corinthians 3:18 says,

> *And we, who with unveiled faces all reflect the Lord's glory, are being transformed into his likeness with ever-increasing glory, which comes from the Lord, who is the Spirit.*

And Philippians 3:20-21 says,

> *But our citizenship is in heaven. And we eagerly await a Savior from there, the Lord Jesus Christ, who, by the power that enables him to bring everything under his control, will transform our lowly bodies so that they will be like his glorious body.*

A friend of mine consistently refers to 1 Peter 1:23,

> *For you have been born again, not of perishable seed, but of imperishable,*

> *through the living and enduring word of God.*

I could substitute the words undying or indestructible for the word imperishable. What is this indestructible seed? It is the Spirit of God. When the word of God was preached to you, and you believed on the Lord Jesus Christ, the Spirit of God came to reside in your heart. God does not die or decay, and therefore, since He has placed imperishable seed in believers, that is His Spirit, they live eternally, and continue to be shaped and transformed into the image of Christ. When believers struggle, and they all do, or even fall flat on their faces, the Spirit does not die or perish, but continues to thrive and flourish in their lives, especially in those hidden areas difficult to surrender. God thrives in our weakness. Paul said,

> *Therefore I will boast all the more gladly about my weaknesses, so that Christ's power may rest on me... For when I am weak, then I am strong.* [2 Corinthians 12:9-10]

The human heart is similar to a hard surface. When a hard surface cracks, or is broken, water can pour into the break. Likewise, the Spirit of God pours into broken areas of a believer's life, healing and transforming. Without the imperishable seed, we'd all be lost.

In the last few years, I've heard Christians forecast a coming revolution to the body of Christ. In one respect, I agree; radical changes are needed. Yet, in another respect, I completely disagree. For many well-intentioned believers, the revolution entails greater miracles, or a modern day resurrection of Acts. They want God to pour out earth-shaking power, and keep church the way it is.

What many believers fail to grasp and understand

is a revolution is merely an exchange of power. Reigning powers are expelled, and revolutionaries take over. The successors may or may not be any more just than the previous rulers. When a structure is wrong, the same abuses eventually rise again; people are people.

Conversely, a reformation is a structural overhaul. A government or organization is reformed. The American revolutionary war led to the creation of a new "form" of government. Instead of a monarchy like England, the founding fathers established a republic. The American Revolution was in actuality a reformation. The new structure was designed to safeguard against the abuses experienced under English rule. Was, and is democracy full proof? No. But, democracy is far better than the previous form of government.

Centuries ago, Martin Luther and other "reformers" challenged the indulgences and corruption found in the Catholic Church. A reformation occurred, altering the face of the church, as well as the structure. Believers who attend a non-catholic Sunday morning service are reaping the fruit of the reformation 500 years earlier. Yet, if the church is going to be restored to its first century glory and beyond, a radical reformation is now required.

In Matthew 13:47-50, Jesus says,

> *Once again, the kingdom of heaven is like a net that was let down into the lake and caught all kinds of fish. When it was full, the fishermen pulled it up on the shore. Then they sat down and collected the good fish in baskets, but threw the bad away. This is how it will be at the end of the age. The angels will come and separate the wicked from the righteous and throw them into the fiery furnace, where there will be weeping and gnashing of teeth.*

The kingdom of heaven far exceeds the church. God saves people through dreams and visions. He sends angels to do His bidding. God performs signs and wonders. Galaxies belong to Him. Even so, the church is His chief witness upon the earth.

In the parable, the church is the net. A net, when held up, from any point, is completely ineffective. Nets are only effective when flattened out. Within Christendom however, the church has exalted a handful of gifted believers. We have superstars. I know Christians who will drive all day, or catch a flight to hear the man of God. I have. Believers continue to sit, stare, and listen to the anointed few. The vast majority of the body of Christ is atrophying.

A net is reinforced at different junctures by nodes or knots. Consider those knots like a leader; they play an integral part in keeping the body of Christ together. There are no special saints though. Leaders are intimately tied to other believers, shoulder to shoulder, and not separated. If a net is loose with gaps, fish escape. The whole church, meaning each believer participates.

I am not referring to showing up on a Sunday morning, and filling a pew. Every believer is uniquely gifted by God, and therefore plays a vital role and function within the church. When believers are not functioning, or doing what they were created for, the church is less than effective.

The majority of believers must realize they are as significant as any of the so-called superstars. Every believer is a son or a daughter of God. The rest of the body of Christ needs them. A number of Christians don't really believe God could use them in some unique, extraordinary way. Secondly, many leaders, certainly not all of them, have promoted themselves, rather than empowering those around them.

Ephesians 4:7-13 reads:

> *But to each one of us grace has been given as Christ apportioned it. This is why it says: When he ascended on high, he led captives in his train and gave gifts to men. What does he ascended mean except that he also descended to the lower, earthly regions? He who descended is the very one who ascended higher than all the heavens, in order to fill the whole universe. It was he who gave some to be apostles, some to be prophets, some to be evangelists, and some to be pastors and teachers, to prepare God's people for works of service, so that the body of Christ may be built up until we all reach unity in the faith and in the knowledge of the Son of God and become mature, attaining to the whole measure of the fullness of Christ.*

Jesus gave gifts to men, namely; apostles, prophets, evangelists, pastors and teachers…

> *…to prepare God's people for works of service, so that the body of Christ may be built up until we all reach unity in the faith and in the knowledge of the Son of God and become mature, attaining to whole the whole measure of the fullness of Christ.*

I can say with great confidence, most believers are not maturing, or being prepared for works of service. A five-fold minister is not called to showcase their giftings. They are called to help others attain their dreams, and callings. A true five-fold minister is a servant to all.

Scripture says,

> *Your attitude should be the same as that of Christ Jesus: Who, being in the very nature God, did not consider equality with God something to be grasped, but made himself nothing, taking the very nature of a servant, being made in human likeness.*
> [Philippians 2:5-7]

Jesus was the very nature of a servant. Therefore, those graced by him, and called to a ministry role, should act like the Lord Jesus Christ and serve. This mandate includes every Christian, but how much more the leaders, or the five-fold ministers.

Paul also said,

> *Do nothing out of selfish ambition or vain conceit, but in humility consider others better than yourselves. Each of you should look not to your own interests, but also the interests of others.* [Philippians 2:3-4]

Humility is rare today. Super-apostles won't consider a ministry engagement unless guaranteed thousands of dollars, and a portion paid up front. I'm not exaggerating! Others demand upscale accommodations. Big venues are mandatory. Star ministers sport titles like bishop or prophet or even pastor. Business cards are made with titles as well as any letters that can be posted behind their name. Apparently, even superstars need validation.

However, not everyone indulges in excess. A number of five-fold ministers serve out of great personal sacrifice. They continually give. I've attended meetings where no registration fee was charged, and anyone who wanted could attend. Only love offerings were taken.

Five-fold ministry roles are often referred to as offices. Offices are for businesses and politicians. The church is a living, breathing organism connected to the head, Jesus Christ. [Colossians 1:18] A believer's relationship is first and foremost with Christ. They are not required to be under any man or ministry, except the Lord Jesus Christ. Many religious Christians embrace the erroneous "covering" doctrine. Allegedly, rank and file believers must submit to a special saint, like an apostle or a prophet. Here again is the top-down, pyramidal structure. The doctrine is one of control and superiority.

According to the doctrine, the superior saint shields and protects the inferior believer. Scripture does not support the covering doctrine. Hebrews 13:17 has been construed at times,

> *Obey your leaders and submit to their authority. They keep watch over you as men who must give an account. Obey them so that their work will be a joy, not a burden, for that would be of no advantage to you.*

Sure believers should submit to their leaders. They are also required to submit to every other believer. We are told,

> "*Submit to one another out of reverence for Christ.*" [Ephesians 5:21]

Believers are never, never to dominate one another. If someone is walking in great authority, their responsibility is to raise up those around them. Believers are told to consider others better than themselves. [Philippians 2:3-4] Paul, one of the greatest apostles of all time said,

> *"... Christ Jesus came into the world to save sinners--- of whom I am the worst."*
> [1Timothy 1:15]

Another verse they love to quote is 1 Corinthians 12:28,

> *And in the church God has appointed first of all apostles, second prophets, third teachers, then workers of miracles, also those having gifts of healing, those able to help others, those with gifts of administration, and those speaking in different kinds of tongues.*

At first glance, there seems to be a hierarchy. But, if one reads the preceding paragraphs, Paul likens the church to the physical body. He says,

> *If the whole body were an eye, where would the sense of hearing be? If the whole body were an ear, where would the sense of smell be? But in fact God has arranged the parts in the body, every one of them, just as he wanted them to be. If they were all one part, where would the body be? As it is, there are many parts, but one body.*
> [1 Corinthians 12:17-20]

There is no mention of individual superiority in this passage, but discusses individual role and function within a unified body or whole: an eye has a different role than an ear; eyes function by seeing and ears function by hearing. Do some body parts play a more vital role than others?

Yes. If a person doesn't have a liver or a pancreas, they're going to die. Apostles have a vital role within the body of Christ, as do prophets. Pastor, teachers, and evangelist do too. But so do those who administer, or help others, or give. My heart does not lord over my kidneys, but rather, it faithfully pumps blood in order that the rest of the body can properly function.

Believers are intimately connected to the head, the Lord Jesus Christ. A person is not a Christian unless they are connected to Him. [John 15:6] Since believers are in Christ, no other intermediary is needed. They can boldly go to the throne of God, and receive mercy and grace in times of need. [Hebrews 4:16]

The present structure is ineffective. Conferences are geared for masses, and must be staged like a show or a concert. The minister has no intimate contact with people. Occasionally, conferences and seminars are healthy and exciting; believers are given the opportunity to celebrate, and rub shoulders with brothers and sisters in Christ. Or, a special teaching or training is given. Too many believers, however, use conferences as their chief means of equipping, and receiving fresh revelation. Big meetings allow believers to dodge real life issues, or matters of the heart. They may learn to minister, but fail to change.

Supposedly, real ministry training occurs in schools. Traditional seminaries stress academics. Conversely, ministry schools place a premium on "doing the stuff." The problem once again is these schools tend to create dichotomies; clergy/laity or participant/spectator. People who are called to "fulltime" ministry attend seminary or ministry school. Other believers somehow have lesser callings. The reality is each and every believer is called to full time ministry. Nowhere does a believer start and stop being a Christian, or ministering.

If a believer peruses the New Testament, they won't find any ministry schools or seminaries. Perhaps the closest thing to a ministry school is found in Acts 19:9, the lecture hall of Tyrannus. Paul taught and had discussions there for two years. As the scripture says,

> *...all the Jews and Greeks who lived in the province of Asia heard the word of the Lord.* [Acts 19:10]

Where in the New Testament is there a school of prophets? There isn't one. Believers struggle to comprehend they have a far better relationship with God than Moses or Elijah ever had, and for that matter any Old Testament prophet. This is why Jesus said,

> *I tell you the truth: Among those born of women there has not risen anyone greater than John the Baptist; yet he who is least in the kingdom of heaven is greater than he.* [Matthew 11:11]

The Spirit indwells believers, whereas, at best, the Spirit merely rested on the Old Testament greats. [Judges 6:34, 11:29] In fact, the prophets prophesied about our days,

> *...I will pour out my Spirit on all people. Your sons and daughters will prophesy, your old men will dream dreams, your young men will see visions. Even on my servants, both men and women, I will pour out my spirit in those days...* [Joel 2:28-29]

A school of the prophets is a throwback to the old covenant. Back then, God dwelt in the temple and not in the hearts of men.

The church must be restructured in such a way that

everyone participates, not just a special few. Gifts are honed and mature, like anything else, as they're exercised. Will a believer make mistakes? Everyone does. This is why Paul admonished the Corinthians to *weigh carefully* prophesies. [1 Corinthians 14:29] Some prophesies were, and are off. Otherwise, why judge a word? When love is the standard though, believers are patient and forgiving of each other.

Traditional Sunday morning church does not facilitate believers ministering to one another. Size makes all the difference. If a gathering is too big, it is virtually impossible for everyone to participate. Nevertheless, the bible instructs believers to minister,

> *...When you come together, everyone has hymn, a revelation, a tongue, or an interpretation. All of these must be done for the strengthening of the church.*
> [1 Corinthians 14:26]

Scripture implies that "everyone" has something to offer. When the Spirit enters a life, He brings good gifts with Him; not for hoarding, but to bless others. Likewise, the gifting of a brother or a sister builds you up. Giftings manifest, but so do personalities, dreams, hopes, struggles, and hurts. I may not be able to help someone, but perhaps someone else can. If a believer belongs to a small intimate group, they can't hide! Struggles and issues get exposed. Many believers shun intimate gatherings because they're afraid of being found out. Exposure is the best thing that could ever happen to them. Small, intimate gatherings facilitate healings.

Five-fold ministers are called *to prepare God's people for works of service*. At the heart of an apostle, prophet, evangelist, teacher, or pastor is the Father's heart. These "gifts" to the body of Christ are fathers and mothers.

If the minister doesn't possess the Father's heart, then, regardless of giftings, their ministry role must be questioned. The church is filled with prodigals because there are so few spiritual parents. Children need parents. Spiritual parenting far exceeds learning how to prophesy or minister. It also includes character and life lessons. Undoubtedly, the disciples received some of their greatest insights by spending time with Jesus. God intended parents and children to spend time together.

The glory a five-fold minister carries radically affects others. Gary Goodell described the experience like this: if a believer hangs around an apostle, they'll dream; if they hang around a prophet, they'll see much clearer; an evangelist, they'll have a passion for the lost; a teacher, they'll hunger for the word; and a pastor, they'll feel loved and cared for. [Goodell] A five-fold minister rubs off on others. Because of the way God wires someone, they gravitate towards a particular ministry. Ultimately, ministering is easy and fun, and not deep, dark and mysterious. When a believer moves in their gifting, it feels completely natural. They simply must obey the promptings of the Lord.

Like in the New Testament, spiritual parent's disciple their children. They guide, affirm, and correct. Soon, a believer knows their place, and they feel good. Instead of dragging themselves to church, the believer is excited and looks forward to getting together with spiritual family. This is why intimacy is so critical. If the closest someone ever comes to a relationship with a spiritual father is fifteen rows back in a huge sanctuary, they're an orphan.

In a small gathering, with fifteen to twenty people sitting in a circle, people get to know each other. A net-like structure affords believers the opportunity to build relationships. Discipleship is not a program. Rather, discipleship is an intimate relationship between two or more people. A good parent draws forth the greatness in their children.

Scripture is almost silent on church structure. Like most things, God grants us great freedom. God allowed the pyramided, top-down structure of church for centuries. The structure is unsuccessful in producing mature believers.

In his book *Smart World*, Richard Ogle discusses network theory. He points out that as diverse connections are made, a new, original order emerges. [Ogle 80-81] There are no five year plans or projections. It just happens. That's because a network is dynamic, fluid, and constantly growing. Who knows where the evolving network will end up. So should the church be. When diverse believers come together, a brand new fellowship should emerge; something that's unique and different. Believers can meet in a tree or a cave if they want to. They can minister to gangsters or golfers. The new fellowship can follow a God-inspired agenda, or wait for the spontaneous leading of the Spirit. God shows each fellowship His order and purpose for them.

The Corinthians' texts discuss issues surrounding sexual immorality and orderly worship. The Pastoral Epistles of 1&2 Timothy and Titus lay certain foundational guidelines for church leadership and conduct. But really, that's about it. For the present season, there are two critical factors for church structure. One, as alluded to earlier, everyone should participate. [1 Corinthians 14:26] Two is size. If a church gets too large, it becomes clumsy and loses vitality.

In John 21, Jesus appeared to the disciples after his death and resurrection. The disciples returned to fishing after Jesus was crucified. They fished all night, but failed to catch anything. [John 21:3] When Jesus arrived, he told them to cast their net on the right side of the boat. [John

21:6] The disciples caught so many fish the net stretched to capacity. Scripture says,

> "*...It was full of large fish, 153, but even with so many the net was not torn.*"
> [John 21:11]

Why does scripture record 153 fish? I'm sure that's how many fish the disciples caught. Except for fisherman of the day, the number had little meaning. However, scripture is timeless. I believe 153 is the maximum number a church should grow to before it splits off, and starts another fellowship.

Malcolm Gladwell recently wrote two best sellers, *The Tipping Point* and *Blink.* Both books are easy, fascinating reads. The tipping point theory goes like this; little events tilt the overall scheme of things. His research indicated three separate groups used 150 as the maximum number for a basic unit; the military, the Hutterites, and Gore Industries. [Gladwell 179-192] The military found that when a fighting unit exceeded 150 soldiers, it became ineffective. The Hutterites, who are an Anabaptist group, start new churches once they reach 150 believers. Gore Industries designs and manufactures high tech products for a multitude of applications. When a plant expands to 150 employees, another plant is immediately started within a few blocks.

Aren't we talking about 153, and not 150? A church should max out at 150 believers with a pastor, a teacher, and an evangelist equipping; thus 153. Pastors, teachers, and evangelists tend to be more local than apostles and prophets. Pastors nurture and train the flock. Teachers ground believers in the Word. Evangelists guide fellowships into their communities.

Christian leaders often take the perspective evangelists are called to travel, going from city to city holding revival meetings. This perspective is skewed. By and large, churches are weak at reaching their own communities. Most churches want to be the light on the hill, hoping the unsaved mysteriously stagger into their fellowships on a Sunday morning. [Matthew 5:14] What about salt? [Matthew 5:13] Why aren't believers in the streets "seasoning" their neighborhoods and communities? A true evangelist lives for this ministry. The paradigm has to change. Many fellowships die out because they become incestuous. That is, believers embrace those most like themselves. Eventually, conformity rules, and life is strangled.

James Surowicki wrote a book entitled *The Wisdom of Crowds.* In the introduction, he told a story about a lost submarine. [Surowicki XX-XXI] The submarine was lost in the middle of the ocean. The government had no idea where it was. The person in charge of the investigation chose a diverse group of thinkers from various disciplines, rather than specialized submarine experts. The team pulled their information together, and determined the location of the sub within 200 yards of where it was found. The oceans are a huge place. That's pretty amazing!

The same is true of the church. Regardless of age, gender, background, socio-economic status, or whatever, everyone has something to offer which enriches the life of the spiritual family. The greater the diversity, the better.

A believer's most fruitful connections or relationships are loose ones. In other words, relationships which produce the greatest life in a fellowship are not necessarily family members or close friends, but rather, superficial acquaintances like the cashier at the supermarket or the waitress at the café. Loose relationships keep believers from tunneling and getting stuck in a rut. Same old gets same old. Different infuses life.

There are exceptions. Philip the evangelist traveled. [Acts 8:4-25] Pastors and teachers travel too. Scripture also says that God's household, the church, is built upon the foundation of the apostles and prophets. [Ephesians 2:20] Paul said,

> "*I planted the seed, Apollos watered it, but God made it grow.*" [1 Corinthians 3:6]

A primary ministry of apostles is planting seeds or starting churches. Prophets water or encourage and strengthen churches. Why do you think Paul appointed Timothy and Titus as pastors? Paul needed trustworthy believers to care for new churches as he took the gospel to unreached territories. In the book of Acts, the apostles and prophets were roadies and itinerant… Paul, Barnabas, Silas, Peter, John, Apollos, Priscilla and Aquila.

Dick Mills once told me the early church prophets were not allowed to stay more than three months in any one church because their revelatory gifting often captivated believers. [Mills] Undoubtedly, rogue prophets took over fellowships. According to Fox's Book of Martyrs, all the original disciples were martyred, with the exception of John, and some, in far, distant lands. [Forbush]

At the end of the net parable, the fishermen separate the good fish from the bad fish; the angels separate the righteous from the wicked. [Matthew 13:47-50] Today, many believers feel their ministry is to identify "wicked" people, and judge. In the parable, this responsibility was left to the angels. Angels receive their instructions from our Lord.

Believers need to understand something extremely important. Be very careful who you oppose, judge, or decide to throw to the curb. God loves His children. I am His favorite son, as are you. Virtually every person who has sought my downfall has paid dearly. My accusers lost ministries and money. A few experienced debilitating diseases. Relationships crumbled. Let God be the judge.

In the Old Testament, father Abraham gave his wife Sarah to king Abimelech. [Genesis 20:2] Abraham feared Abimelech would kill him for Sarah. [Genesis 20:11] Even though Abraham was wrong, God told Abimelech,

> *Now return the man's wife, for he is a prophet, and he will pray for you and you will live. But if you do not return her, you may be sure that you and all yours will die.* [Genesis 20:7]

Some believers might contend, "That was the Old Testament" or "Abraham was a prophet." There is a deeper principle here though. First of all, Abraham was special. However, believers have a better covenant with God than Abraham ever possessed. Secondly, a believer may not be a full blown prophet, but every believer is prophetic because,

> "*...the testimony of Jesus is the spirit of prophecy.*" [Revelation 19:10]

Every believer carries the testimony of Jesus. God protects and defends His sons and daughters, even when His children are wrong. A good father never disowns or stops loving his children because of their misbehavior. God protects us from spiritual siblings as well as others.

Another contention is "God would never put a disease on someone, or remove a ministry." The most important thing to God is a person's heart. He allows people to face hardship and difficulties in order that their hearts might yield to Him. Paul challenged the Corinthians to turn an immoral brother over to Satan so his sinful nature could be destroyed. [1 Corinthians 5:5] I'm thankful for every correction in my life; the mercies of God have sustained me.

How can believers be so arrogant as to deem certain people good, and others as evil or unredeemable. As I survey the life of Jesus, He never shunned anybody. His presence stirred darkness wherever He went; the light exposed the hidden. Does your presence agitate the oppressed or the religious? Or, are you simply "fixing" others, and looking for the speck in their eye? Are you a spiritual policeman? Jesus knew Judas Iscariot's character and destiny, yet he never excluded him. [John 6:71, 12:4]

The parable of the mustard seed states,

> *The kingdom of heaven is like a mustard seed, which a man took and planted in his field. Though it is the smallest of all your seeds, yet when it grows, it is the largest of the garden plants and becomes a tree, so that the birds of the air come and perch in its branches.* [Matthew 13:31-32]

The mustard seed represents the church. It is the smallest of seeds. Likewise, Jesus began the church with a handful of misfits. The mustard seed grew like a tree. The church spread throughout the earth. The birds of the air came and perched in the branches. Satan is depicted as the ruler of the air. [Ephesians 2:2] In Revelation 18:2, evil spirits are likened to unclean birds. In this parable, the birds of the air represent demonic entities. Sadly, the demonic finds rest and shade in the church. Some of the worst evil is found in the church, especially at the top of the pyramid. Through illegitimate satanic authority, a multitude of church leaders have crushed many of God's children. Jeremiah 23:1 says,

Woe to the shepherds who are destroying and scattering the sheep of my pasture! Declares the Lord.

Let God determine who is good and bad. Don't judge!
Listen to what Jesus says,

Love your enemies, do good to those who hate you, bless those who curse you, pray for those who mistreat you. [Luke 6:27-28]

Believers are called to love their enemies. The Christian standard is to give back goodness for evil and blessings for curses. Jesus lived this way, and so must His church.

THE LANGUAGE OF THE SPIRIT

Oh yes I can make it now the pain is gone
All of the bad feelings have disappeared
Here is that rainbow I've been praying for
It's gonna be a bright bright, bright, bright sun shiny day
JOHNNY NASH *I CAN SEE CLEARLY NOW*

Good communication is the currency of meaningful relationships. Frustration and anger are produced when people cannot communicate with each other.

I had an irritating experience while traveling overseas. In Paris, France I rode the underground. Late one night, a friend and I were confused and missed our stop. A couple of Parisians sat next to me. When I asked for help in English, they wouldn't even look at me. I found myself incensed. Apparently, all the nasty things I'd heard about the French were true. Fortunately for us, a Good Samaritan was on board. A Frenchman in his early to mid-thirties stood across from us, reading. He looked up, and asked me in English where we needed to go. The Good Samaritan skipped his stop, and rode with us until we reached our destination. I'm sure he went a good forty-five minutes out of his way just to help us. When people ask me what I think of the French, I tell them they're some of the nicest people in the world.

Riding the underground in France, and living in France are two different things. If I lived in France, I would be expected to learn French. Conversely, if a Frenchman moved to America, we would expect him to learn English. Each person is hardwired for language and communication, and so these expectations are not unreasonable.

Our Spirits are made for spiritual communication. Just like learning any natural language requires effort and discipline, so does learning the language of the Spirit. Everyone is capable. In God's kingdom, the language of the Spirit is spoken. Believers are citizens of His kingdom. [Philippians 3:20] God expects His citizens to learn the language.

When I was first involved in ministry, I heard a few believers say things like, "God told me…" or "I heard the Lord say…" I found myself extremely frustrated. Did they hear an audible voice? Or, was there a voice in their heads? How did they know God was speaking? Gradually, through trial and error, I began to know the voice of God. Ever since then, I've continued to hone and refine my communication skills, and I probably always will.

Many believers have had a similar experience. This chapter will help prevent frustration and discouragement from setting in. Regardless of who the believer is though, they will still occasionally miss what God is communicating. Everyone does, and that's okay. God is first and foremost our loving Father.

I begin by discussing spiritual senses; these are even more real than the natural senses. Next, I explain the role of ministering spirits or angels. I then clarify how the Holy Spirit, Jesus, and the heavenly Father communicate with believers. Throughout, I provide personal experience to highlight points.

When people are awake, and up and going, they

cannot help but see and hear. They might see the stove on, or where to turn when driving. Perhaps they hear the beep of the microwave, or the news on the radio. Nobody taught them to see or to hear; either a person sees and hears, or they don't. For most people, seeing and hearing is very natural. Even so, with all the external stimulation, people turn off and tune out inconsequential sights and sounds. The hum of the refrigerator is no longer heard, and the cat on the fence is ignored. People focus on things pertinent to their lives. They're still seeing and hearing, however, they've become selective. Physical senses are extensions of a person's spirit.

Paul said,

> "*I pray also that the eyes of your heart may be enlightened....*" [Ephesians 1:18]

As scripture indicates, the heart or the spirit has eyes.

Jesus said over and over again to the seven churches in the book of Revelation,

> "*He who has an ear, let him hear what the Spirit says to the churches.*" [Revelation 2:7]

Everyone has ears. Yet, to hear what the Spirit is saying requires "spiritual ears." Paul goes on to say,

> *The man without the Spirit does not accept the things that come from the Spirit of God, for they are foolishness to him, and he cannot understand them, because they are spiritually discerned.* [1 Corinthians 2:14]

In other words, spiritual realities require spiritual hearing; other-wise, they sound foolish or make little sense.

Hebrews 5:12-14 says,

> *In fact, though by this time you ought to be teachers, you need someone to teach you the elementary truths of God's word all over again. You need milk, not solid food! Anyone who lives on milk, being still an infant, is not acquainted with the teaching about righteousness. But solid food is for the mature, who by constant use have trained themselves to distinguish good from evil.*

Here, scripture is talking about food, and in order to partake of food, taste is a faculty. Or, is scripture merely using metaphorical or poetic language? The bible does. Nevertheless, believers can spiritually taste, and for that matter; hear, see, smell, and feel too.

Scripture also says,

> *Then Noah built an alter to the Lord and, taking some of all the clean animals and birds, he sacrificed burnt offerings on it. The Lord smelled the pleasing aroma...*
> [Genesis 8:20-21]

I doubt if the Lord found the natural smell of burnt animals pleasing. Years ago, as a boy, I worked cattle. Sometimes we branded cattle all day long, and it stunk! Noah and his family's sacrifice had a fragrant "spiritual" aroma to the Lord.

And Jeremiah said,

> *But if I say, I will not mention him or speak any more in his name, his word is in my heart like fire, a fire shut up in my bones. I*

am weary of holding it in; indeed, I cannot.
[Jeremiah 20:9]

Jeremiah could "feel" the word of God burning in him.

Most people, believers and unbelievers alike, can recall strange or weird experiences. Perhaps they walked into a room and saw a shadow in the corner, or felt uneasy around a certain person. Maybe they heard a comment that wasn't said. These types of experiences, and others like them, are often spiritual. A person unknowingly senses with their spirits. Folks attribute the experience to coincidence or tiredness because they were never taught to use their spiritual senses. Like natural senses, spiritual senses must be trained and focused too.

An infant is captivated by virtually everything. They bounce around, handling and tasting whatever they can latch onto. As a person matures, they learn to concentrate on points of interest or concern. Believers do the same thing in the spirit. When a believer becomes aware of their spiritual selves, and use their spiritual senses, they become hyper-spiritual; every little event or happening catches their attention. As the believer grows in the Lord, they're not so easily distracted. Spiritual trivia flutters bye.

A number of ministries provide outstanding teachings and trainings on revelatory skills. However, a few of these ministries continue to propagate the erroneous doctrine of "levels." Supposedly, as a believer progresses on their spiritual journey, they attain new levels or new plateaus of understanding. This doctrine led to the development of elaborate revelatory systems. For example, an open vision is greater than a dream, and an audible voice supersedes an impression. The spiritually immature use these types of experiences to bolster their own insecurities. The levels doctrine is a throwback to western hierarchal thinking.

The biblical paradigm is intimacy. Believers have a heavenly Father, and therefore, as sons and daughters, they do not work or labor for their relationship with Him. Orphans strive and search, but sons and daughters belong. Believers are children of God.

Consider very intimate relationships; father and son, mother and daughter, or husband and wife. I'll use my wife as an example. Because I love my wife, I spend as much time with her as possible. My relationship with her is not laborious or difficult, but rather, it's a joy. I know her better than anyone else, except God. Even when my wife is not speaking, she is still communicating. Her facial expressions and posture speaks volumes to me. I know what makes her happy and what hurts her. She tells me her hopes and dreams. I can pick her voice out in a crowd. My wife has a very distinct scent; it's beautiful. She likes romantic movies, and hot & spicy foods. Since I'm very intimate with my wife, I could go on and on. Greater intimacy equals greater knowledge of each other.

Now, consider your relationship with God. Do you love to spend time with Him? Can you say, like Jesus, you only do what you see the Father doing? [John 5:19] Do you know what pleases your Father, and what hurts Him? Does He share His heart with you? Can you pick God's voice out in a crowd? Can you smell Him in a room? These are revealing questions. Yet, every believer is called to a deep, meaningful relationship with God. Our relationship with the Lord should surpass all others. God intimately knows each and every believer, but each and every believer is called to intimately know Him; more than anyone else.

Many believers struggle with intimacy because of a distorted view of God. Absent and abusive fathers have left a multitude of believers scarred and damaged. Ministers reinforce the distortion by portraying the heavenly Father as a mean, old tyrant who looks for opportunities to throw sinful people into hell. Countless believers are terrified of God. Fear retards intimacy.

There is the other end of the spectrum too. God is portrayed as a doting, old grandfather who jumps every time his children want something. Few believers are called to handle billions of dollars, or own a personal jet. Here, believers fail to respect the greatness of the Father. If fear retards intimacy, then arrogance cheapens it.

God is not mean and hateful, nor is He a sugar daddy. Our Father is consistently portrayed as something He's not. He is the most loving Father anyone could ever imagine. The Father corrects, disciplines, blesses, generously gives, protects, laughs, cries, rejoices, coddles, challenges, patiently waits, believes, and shares with all His children. Above all else, however, the Father loves being alone with each child.

Everyone has a sensory predisposition. Some students learn through hearing. They are auditory people. Craftsmen and mechanics handle things; they're tactile. Others are visually inclined, and enjoy photography and movies. Take a couple of moments and reflect. Consider school, hobbies, and even frustrations. Patterns are probably surfacing. People are spiritually inclined too. Most believers primarily see, hear, or feel. Which is best? That's the wrong question. The appropriate question is, "How does God communicate with you?" For me, I see things. I close my physical eyes because I want to see with the eyes of my heart. Images flash before me. Occasionally though, my eyes are open and an image is seemingly placed between me and my natural surroundings.

Although believers are predisposed or inclined to a particular spiritual sense, the other senses function and should be developed as well. I've walked into rooms and smelled a fresh, spring-like fragrance; it was the presence of the Lord. Conversely, while ministering deliverance, the stench of rotten eggs filled a room. One or two conversations left a bitter taste in my mouth.

A friend of mine hears very clearly, and says, "I hear the Lord saying…" And still others feel things in the pit of their stomachs; it's like a spiritual meter or sensor goes off in their cores. Sometimes, these folks can't articulate what their sensing. They simply know if the circumstances are good or bad. This gifting is called discernment. My wife functions this way.

As believers press into their relationship with the Lord, they begin to recognize His presence or voice. Soon, the Lord's voice becomes very distinct. Elijah hid in a cave. [1 Kings 19:9-18] A wind, an earthquake, and a fire all passed in front of the cave, but Elijah knew the Lord was not in them. After the fire, however, came a gentle whisper. [1 Kings 19:12] Elijah knew the gentle whisper was the Lord.

There are a multitude of voices competing for the attention of every believer. The sources include one's self, the demonic, people, and of course the Lord. Some folks are horribly deceived. This is why Jeremiah said, "*The heart is deceitful above all things.*" [Jeremiah 17:9]

Believers confuse their voice with God's. The confusion originates in the flesh. The deceived want something so much they become convinced God spoke to them. They use the phrase, "The Lord told me…" When these folks use this phrase, they are saying in so many words, "Don't challenge me." I feel the religious, self-righteousness emanating from them. This flavor of deception generally promotes self-aggrandizement.

If a believer heard a voice instructing them to murder their neighbor, they would absolutely know the voice was not God's. The instructions completely contradict scripture. However, as one moves from black and white, that is clear and distinct, to shades of grey, voices become much more difficult to distinguish. Satan masquerades as an angel of light. [2 Corinthians 11:14] His words are not always unbiblical, and often times, he is very cunning and seductive, even using scripture to his own ends. Satan used scripture to tempt Jesus in the desert. [Luke 4:10-11] He sometimes speaks through people. [Matthew 16:23] I've seen faces and demeanors change all of sudden, like a switch was thrown. Anybody can be used by Satan including your wife, husband, children and closest friends. Even you!

Believers must never stray from scripture. Once again, if a voice contradicts scripture, God is not speaking. Read His word! Next, consider what affect a voice has on you. Does the voice cause pride? Is it glorifying someone other than God? Does the voice instill fear? Confusion? Hopelessness? Condemnation or guilt? God's voice always draws the believer closer to Him, even in correction.

Friends ministered to me years ago, and they came against double-mindedness. Few believers want correction, and I'm no exception. Nevertheless, the rebuke was sweet because the Lord was the Author. My relationship deepened with God.

I've known ministries who ranted and raved, working themselves up. Supposedly, if they're loud enough, and they get the tingles, then the Lord is present and He hears them. These antics remind me of the prophets of Baal. Scripture says,

> *Then they called on the name of Baal from morning till noon. O Baal answer us! they shouted. But there was no response; no one answered. And they danced around the alter they had made... So they shouted*

> *louder and slashed themselves with swords and spears, as was their custom, until their blood flowed. Midday passed, and they continued their frantic prophesying until the time for the evening sacrifice. But there was no response, no one answered, no one paid attention.* [1 Kings 18:26, 28-29]

God is not hard of hearing, nor is He blind. The Lord is ever present through His Spirit. [Hebrews 13:5] I'm all for praying in tongues, and worshipping with passionate abandonment. However, if a believer wants to commune with the Lord there is a better way.

When I want to spend time with a special person, like my wife, I avoid loud, busy places. My focus is her, and because I passionately love my wife, I spend more time listening than speaking; I want her and all she has to offer.

Here's the first step in hearing the Lord. Dial down. Turn off the TV and the computer. Get alone. Go for a drive or a walk. Sit at the kitchen table with a cup of coffee. The crucial factor is getting alone. Being alone can be scary. I know people who are addicted to stimulation, and they're terrified of quiet. Remember, however, you're never alone; God will never leave you nor forsake you. He's waited for you. God wants to be with you and you alone.

Share your heart. Let Him know your thoughts and feelings. Ask the Father to speak. He will, and expect it. God is closer to you than you are to yourself.

The difficulty lies in listening. Close your eyes, and remain quiet. God immediately responds. You might have an impression, or hear a soft gentle voice. Perhaps a picture comes to mind. God could direct your attention to nature. If you're experiencing something demeaning or hurtful, it's not God. Take authority over the lying voice in Jesus name, and bind it. Speak out loud. Conversely, God's voice brings life, and builds up. He loves His children.

Don't analyze the Lord's response. People are apt to grind things through their minds. Just listen. Thank God for speaking. Continue the process. Respond to Him, and listen again. Generally, believers find the whole experience exhilarating. Communing with the Lord can occur anywhere, anytime; work, home, driving, or exercising to name a few. Nothing, absolutely nothing, can separate the believer from God. [Romans 8:38-39]

Communion not only enables the believer to hear the voice of God, but also to abide in the Spirit. Jesus said, "*Remain in me, and I will remain in you.*" [John 15:4] He also said,

> *And I will ask the Father, and he will give another Counselor to be with you forever – the Spirit of truth.* [John 14:16-17]

Believers can live moment to moment in God. Yet, sometimes, nothing is said by God or the believer. My wife and I, while on long walks or drives, will occasionally not say a word. We aren't fighting. Rather, her presence is enough. God is like that too. Just knowing He is always with me is enough.

Distractions come from everywhere. Abiding in the Spirit requires great effort. The chief strategy for Spirit living is hiding away with the Lord. Make alone time routine. Scripture says,

> *Very early in the morning, while it was still dark, Jesus got up, left the house and went to a solitary place, where he prayed.*
> [Mark 1:35]

What Jesus did, believers are called to do. Intimacy with the Lord is the greatest ministry of all.

Couples who have stood the test of time and remained married, tell me their relationships are the best they've ever been. As their marriages matured, so has their intimacy. All meaningful relationships are founded on love. Love is expressed through intimacy. The more love, the greater the intimacy. After a while, not only does one communicate with their beloved, but they know their ways: values, likes and dislikes, pet-peeves, reactions, expectations, and more.

The bible says the two become one. [Genesis 2:24] I've heard that couples who have been married for years look like each other. Husbands and wives are confused for brothers and sisters. Death and divorce are so painful because a spouse loses part of themselves.

Yet, the Lord never leaves us. If we are faithless, He is faithful. [2 Timothy 2:13] As a believer regularly spends time with the Lord, not only does their communication mature, but, they learn God's ways too.

Moses asked the Lord to teach him His ways. [Exodus 33:13] Through seasons of relationship, the intimate believer learns the ways of God. While others wonder what God is doing, the intimate believer knows. Like an old married couple, lovers of God look like Him. The bible states,

> *And we, who with unveiled faces all reflect the Lord's glory,* are *being transformed into his likeness with ever-increasing glory, which comes from the Lord, who is the Spirit.* [2 Corinthians 3:18]

Scripture says angels are ministering spirits. Hebrews 1:14 reads,

> *"Are not all angels ministering spirits sent to serve those who will inherit salvation?"*

What are angels like? Hebrews 13:2 says,

> *Do not forget to entertain strangers, for by so doing some people have entertained angels without knowing it.*

Angels take on human form. In Acts 12 the church was persecuted. Peter was imprisoned, and later freed by an angel. [Acts 12:3-4, 7-10] Aware of Peter's imprisonment, the church interceded. When Peter miraculously showed up, the believers thought it was his angel. [Acts 12:15] The western, modern church doesn't think this way. [Fenn] In the same situation, we would undoubtedly believe the person is Peter. For the ancient oriental mind, however, angels were normal, and a part of everyday life.

Angels are sent by God to minister to the needs and callings of believers. When angels speak, it is always external. Their communication is specific or exacting. For example, angels were explicit in their instructions to Lot and his family. [Genesis 19:17-22] Cornelius the centurion received specific instructions from an angel too. [Acts 10:4-6]

Once, while lying in bed, I heard an audible voice say, "Confidence!" I was supposed to give a prophetic word that morning to a large group of believers, but, I was scared. In the end, I chickened out. Even so, I knew my angel spoke the word "confidence." Although I couldn't see him, I sensed his presence. He stood by my bed. Nowadays, when I see a flash or a spark of light, I know an angel is present. However, if I close my eyes, and dial down, I see them much better, clearer.

I've had other distinct encounters too. On one

occasion, I was out with an old high school friend. While at a bar, a couple of girls stole his credit card. They thought the prank was funny. I grabbed one by the jacket, and told her to give the card back. In the next moment, a big guy was shouting my name and charging me. He wasn't rushing over to chit-chat. A young man, whom I'd never seen before, stepped between us, and started fighting him. Bouncers ran toward us. I decided I'd better leave, and slipped out. I'm convinced my angel saved me from a beating that night, or something worse.

After my second divorce, I went riding late one evening. I stopped at a seedy, little bar, and had a beer. A thirty-something gal approached me, and said she and her friend wanted to party. Both women were married. They wanted to go to another bar, and I thought to myself, "Why not?" When I got on my bike to follow, I heard an audible voice say, "If you go, you'll die." I was scared to death. I rode straight home. The following day, I knew I had to sell my bike, and I did. I cried. Once again, my angel saved me.

When I close my eyes, and focus, I see my angel. He is grey like steel, very handsome, and about six feet tall. His name is Swift. True to his name, Swift is extremely fast, and powerful.

There is great controversy concerning angels. Some believers are captivated with angels, and deify them. Others are fearful of sliding into New Age ideology, and therefore, limit angels to spiritual body guards. Believers are not to worship angels. In Revelation, John encounters one of these regal beings face to face, and falls down to worship him. Scripture says,

> *At this I fell at his feet to worship him. But he said to me, 'Do not do it! I am a fellow servant with you and with your brothers who hold to the testimony of Jesus. Worship*

> *God! For the testimony of Jesus is the spirit of prophecy.* [Revelation 19:10]

Believers worship God, and not angels.

In 2 Thessalonians 2:9-10 it says,

> *The coming of the lawless one will be in accordance with the work of Satan displayed in all kinds of counterfeit miracles, signs and wonders, and every sort of evil that deceives those who are perishing.*

For there to be counterfeit, there must be genuine. If Satan, a fallen created being has power to perform miracles, so do God's angelic host. God, by His very nature is diverse, and seemingly, His angelic order is diverse too. Angels restore and heal. [1 Kings 19:5-9] They kill. [2 Chronicles 32:21] Deliver messages. [Luke 1:11-20] Protect. [Psalm 34:7] Obviously, angels perform a multitude of tasks on behalf of believers.

Why the distinctions? Communication is an art. Children have undeveloped, limited palates. Given the choice between lamb or veal and macaroni and cheese, most children choose macaroni and cheese. Chicken fingers and French fries are another favorite. As people grow and mature, their palates become more sophisticated; they can enjoy something that's not deep fried or smothered in ketchup. Diversity adds richness.

Believer's communication with God is similar. As they mature, their relationship with the Lord takes on nuances and shades. Communication grows, and it should. God speaks in unique ways to bring greater clarity, but also to add flavor and intensity to the relationship. As believers understand how the Father communicates, the better they know Him. Should anything take precedence over one's relationship with God? Greater love means greater intimacy. The more one knows the Lord, the more they love Him.

Scripture says of the Holy Spirit,

> *But when he, the Spirit of truth, comes, he will guide you into all truth. He will speak not on his own; he will speak only what he hears, and he will tell you what is yet to come. He will bring glory to me by taking from what is mine and making it known to you.* [John 16:12-14]

The Holy Spirit is God within believers. The voice of the Spirit is extremely detailed and internal. He illuminates all of life, and empowers believers to truly see. If believers relax and listen, the Spirit guides them into all truth.

Through the years, the Spirit has revealed precise information to me. He's given specific names, present situations, as well as past and future events. Like all believers, my only limitation has been myself. The Spirit imparts revelation for life, and not destruction.

Believers confuse the voice of the Holy Spirit with their own. A strange thought enters their mind, and they think, "Where did that come from?" or "Nah, that's just me." Some of the strangest thoughts and images originate with the Spirit.

I remember ministering to a little gal from Texas. I asked the Lord to speak. Instantaneously, I saw a picture of a young UPS driver delivering a package. I thought to myself; "I really need to focus. My mind is wondering." The picture kept recurring. I finally shared the image with the Texan. She wept. Her son was trying to get a job with United Parcel Service.

When believers ask God something, He responds;

it's His character. The Father does not subject His children to the silent treatment. I've heard believers say, "God will speak when He wants." or "Who are you? God doesn't have to speak to you." These believers came from hurtful, broken homes and project their past onto God. Why wouldn't the Father reply? He's living in us. God has always answered me. Occasionally, His response isn't pleasant, but that's the nature of truth. Even so, God speaks to His children.

In the book of Revelation, John said he was in the Spirit. [Revelation 1:10] Today, believers can be caught up in the Spirit too. While lying in bed late one night, all of sudden, I found myself sitting on a stool in the hallway. My deceased grandmother, Esther, and a little old lady whom I'd met in Italy, walked by me and into my bedroom. I got up, and followed them. I saw myself sleeping in bed. The two stood over me and gently stroked my head. Each lady, but especially my grandma, had a kind, endearing expression on their face. And then the experience ended as quickly as it began.

Many believers are under the strong delusion that deceased saints are merely enjoying heavenly mansions. Not so! We are being cheered on by those who have gone on before us; some we don't even know. Hebrews 12:1 says,

> *Therefore, since we are surrounded by such a great cloud of witnesses, let us throw off everything that hinders and the sin that so easily entangles, and let us run with perseverance the race marked out for us.*

A close friend and I ministered at a reservation. On one occasion, we were there during the Christmas season. A number of folks wanted ministry. Time was running out though; a scheduled family dinner was four and a half hours away. Should we stay, or go? We ministered to everyone. The best thing to do was forget the dinner.

We finally left. Time seemingly stopped. What should have taken four and a half hours of hard driving, took only two and a half hours of easy driving. Whole stretches of the familiar road disappeared. We arrived right on time.

I always wanted a Philip-like translation, and the Lord gave me one. The experience was nothing like I expected. Our translation was strangely natural and effortless.

Jesus visits people too. When Paul was on the road to Damascus, Jesus came to him. [Acts 9:3-6] He also appeared to John on the island of Patmos. [Revelation 1:9-11]

Romans 8:34-35 says,

> *Who is he that condemns? Christ Jesus, who died – more than that, who was raised to life – is at the right hand of God and is also interceding for us. Who shall separate us from the love of Christ?*

Intercession is not only Jesus going before the Father on our behalf, but also, Jesus coming to us on behalf of the Father. He draws people back to God. His ministry has never changed. What Jesus did, he continues to do.

When Jesus is near, I'm overwhelmed with compassion and love. Scripture says,

> *When he saw the crowds, he had compassion on them, because they were harassed and helpless, like sheep without a shepherd.* [Matthew 9:36]

While having a meeting at my parent's home, Jesus came. I couldn't stop weeping. Jesus moved from one end of the room to the other, and as he moved, people were methodically touched and healed; a skin irritation disappeared, an injured knee flexed, sight cleared, a heart improved, and back pain left.

My grandma received a healing. Over her ninety plus years, grandma's heart weakened. She routinely saw a cardiologist. On her next check-up, after the meeting, the cardiologist said her heart had dramatically improved. We knew why.

Jesus visited me in Canada too. As I prayed with a group of pastors for the community, I felt a hand resting on my shoulder. I turned to see who was there, and no one was, yet, the hand continued to rest on my shoulder. Once again, I wept. I experienced the love of Jesus for our community.

Believers struggle with the notion of personally engaging the heavenly Father. In the Old Testament, people were smitten dead if they improperly approached God. [Leviticus 10:1-3] Yet, with the sacrifice of Jesus, believers are seated with Him in the heavenly realms. [Ephesians 2:6] And, where is Jesus? He is at the right hand of the Father. [Romans 8:34] Believers, then, are even now before the Father. The New Testament reality is believers are thoroughly righteous because of the atoning work of Jesus Christ. [2 Corinthians 5:21]

Is there scriptural support for the Father walking amongst us? God walked with Adam and Eve in the Garden of Eden. [Genesis 3:8] Again, the work of Jesus has returned believers to a blameless state. The Lord also visited Moses and Elijah. [Exodus 24:15-17, 1 Kings 19:11-13]

When the Father came to me, I was completely undone. Late one evening, I got up to pray. The presence of the Father was in the room, and I froze, like a statue.

I couldn't move. Revelation poured into me; I understood situations at church, in the lives of others, and in my own life. I was in awe and wanted more, but, I was also terrified and wanted to run, all at the same time. The experience lasted for about a half hour. Afterwards, I went back to bed exhausted, and slept.

Peter quotes Joel in Acts 2:17-18,

> *In those days, God says, I will pour out my Spirit on all people. Your sons and daughters will prophesy, your young men will see visions, and your old men will dream dreams. Even on my servants, both men and women, I will pour out my spirit in those days, and they will prophesy.*

God speaks through dreams and visions. The Holy Spirit does the work, but the Father initiates and directs.

Dreams can't be altered; they are what they are. The problem arises, however, in determining meaning. Dreams can be actual, or symbolic. They clarify the past, illuminate the present, and forewarn the future.

Years ago, I started and pastured a small denominational church in eastern Canada. We were very successful; heavily involved in the community, off subsidy, raising leaders, two worship teams, starting another church, and so on. However, the church lacked a missions program. We decided to focus on the Mugali people; there was not one known Christian among them. They lived in an isolated mountainous region in Nepal, near the Chinese border. The Mugali's were Tibetan Buddhists.

Four of us were chosen to scout Nepal. While there, we experienced great favor and divine connections. Upon our arrival home, we shared the good news with the others. The church was excited.

After a year or two, things unraveled. Each trekker suffered hardship; two of us got divorced, one went bankrupt, and another was diagnosed with ovarian cancer. Later, the Lord revealed what happened through a dream.

Dream: I was Asian with almond shaped eyes, dark skin, and black hair. Three other Asians were with me. We hotly pursued a fifth. Everyone had superhuman powers. We flew over buildings, went through walls, and even tossed cars aside. Our target stopped running, and fought. One by one, he killed off the others. I was last. We were in an ancient, stone building. Jesus was there too. He sat peacefully on a bench and watched. At first,
I held my own. I slowly started losing though. I found myself very angry with Jesus. I thought, "Why don't you help me?" Then, my adversary killed me, and I fell dead. As soon as I hit the ground, blood covered my feet, and started moving up my entire body, until I was completely engulfed. All of a sudden, I came back to life. **End of dream.**

Interpretation of dream: Our ethnicity indicated we were battling a foreign principality. When challenged, the principality destroyed us. The superhuman powers demonstrated our struggle was spiritual, and not natural. Jesus allowed my death, but resurrected me.

We defeated ourselves. Each believer was "hooked." The principality was aware of those areas in our lives that were not surrendered to the Lord. He found our weaknesses and then exploited them. My dream explained the past.

God has warned me through dreams too. Once, while riding downtown, I met a very interesting, and beautiful woman. She was a massage therapist, rode bikes, made biscuits and gravy, and wanted to go boar hunting. Wow! She gave me her phone number, and we agreed to have coffee in a couple of days. The following evening I had a dream.

Dream: I stood next to an open door in a hotel lobby or a banquet hall. The door led to a room filled with sixty or seventy couples. Everyone was happy. On the inside of the door was a heart, and written inside the heart was the number 250. Whenever a couple walked by, I urged them to enter. I was proselytizing marriage. **End of dream.**

Interpretation of dream: As a rule, I only use my NIV Study bible. It's worn and beat-up, scribbled in, and taped together. The number 250 was seared in my mind.
I turned to page 250 in my bible. I had underlined, "*You shall not covet your neighbor's wife.*" I called my date, and asked her if she was married. She was. God revealed the truth through a dream.

I had some very unusual dreams while living in Montana. One was disturbingly real.

Dream: I and another person crouched in thick brush.
I don't know who the other person was though. A strange creature stood in the distance. The creature was half human, and half bear. The head and shoulders were furry, and looked like a bear. From the shoulders down, however, the body was a naked, voluptuous woman.
I held a hunting rifle. My companion said, "Shoot it. Shoot it." I replied, "I don't know what it is." And I didn't. Was it human, or a bear? The creature heard us arguing, and attacked before I could fire a shot. I wrestled with it on the ground. I started winning, and found myself on top. A park ranger stood over us, and watched. I urged the ranger to give me his gun. He handed me his pistol, and I shot the creature in the chest. The ranger said, "You killed it." I replied, "No I didn't. You have to shoot it in the head." I then shot the creature in the head. **End of dream.**

Two days after the dream, my prayer partner was startled in the early morning hours. Her dog went crazy. She opened the back door, and saw a black bear in her yard. She shut the door, and grabbed her rifle. Next, the bear shoved against the Plexiglas porch door terrorizing her dog. When she opened the back door again, the bear looked at her, backed up, and charged. She shot through the porch door, and struck the bear in the head. It fell, but got up, and she shot it again. The bear crawled down the steps and died. I spent half a day gutting and skinning a bear. This black bear was the largest Fish and Game had seen in the area for years, weighing well over 400 pounds.

Interpretation of dream: The creature was an image of the evil powers at work in the community. The body represented Jezebel; it was feminine and seductive. The bear's head was "over" Jezebel, and ruled the area. Bears represent death; they maul, kill, and devour. Death was the real power, and Jezebel was the underling.

Believers rant and rave about Jezebel. Without a doubt, she's a force which wrecks havoc throughout the church and the world. Yet, Jezebel is not even a general in the kingdom of darkness. To destroy the work of Jezebel, Death had to be dealt with. Our prayers and intercession stirred up a dangerous, physical manifestation of Death.

During a vision, a person's eyes are open. A spiritual picture or movie is superimposed over natural settings. Pictures and images can convey messages that words fail to adequately express.

Vision: I prayed in the Spirit as I lay in bed. Suddenly, the vaulted ceiling became a movie screen. A giant, ominous eagle perched at one end of the ceiling. Hundreds of black and brown horses appeared at the other end, and raced toward the eagle. Dust flew everywhere. The horses were riled, and bent on harm. The eagle reared, slashing and clawing. Each horse vaporized. New horses materialized, and instantly charged. They were destroyed too. The vision lasted for minutes, but felt like an eternity. I couldn't stand it anymore, and cried out the name of Jesus. **End of vision.**

Interpretation of vision: A couple of years later, while I sat in a plane, the Lord explained the vision. The eagle represented Jesus. The black horses signified spiritual battles, and the brown horses earthly battles. My Father told me Jesus would fight my spiritual and earthly battles, and I would prevail.

I had that vision over twenty years ago. Jesus has protected me all these years, and through everything I've encountered. A few times I've been knocked down, and even fallen, nevertheless, I've prevailed. Scripture says in Romans 8:31,

> *"What, then, shall we say in response to this? If God is for us, who can be against us"*

And Proverbs 24:16 says,

> *...for though a righteous man falls seven times, he rises again, but the wicked are brought down by calamity.*

Vision: Once again, I was in bed. As I prayed, my eyes were supernaturally opened. I saw strange looking beings floating around the room. Most were like distorted humans or weird animals; their body parts were exaggerated. For example, one entity looked like a fish, but had a long, bizarre nose. I knew this creature swam into people's life, and "snooped" around, causing suspicion amongst friends and family. I saw demons. They were not frightful or intimidating, only ugly. I then focused my eyes on a demon, like a gun, and said, "In Jesus Name." Bam! The demons disappeared. **End of vision**.

Interpretation of vision: The interpretation is obvious and straightforward: Believers in the Lord Jesus Christ have authority over demons.

Each and every believer is unique and wonderfully made, and therefore, God communicates with us according to who we are as a person. God may speak to you in ways He would never speak to me. The beauty of each relationship with the Lord is personal intimacy. Besides your heart condition, intimacy with the Lord is the most critical factor in overcoming. If you will listen to the Lord, He will walk you through every battle and obstacle you encounter.

EPILOGUE

Like everyone else, I'm in process. Through the Lord Jesus Christ, I overcame hardships and difficulties. Even so, most of my problems originated in me. Since there are so few clear voices, I've found myself in quandaries, and learned the hard way. My heart's desire is to be a clear voice for others, and save them the grief I've experienced.

Teachers read books on teaching, and leaders on leading. You read a book on overcoming. Hopefully this book spoke to your heart. If no one has ever told you this before, I am. *You're an overcomer. You belong to the fellowship of ghosts.*

I began this book with a dream, and I'll finish with one too. Just the other night, the Lord gave me a profound dream.

Dream: I stood on a wooden dock with a red rototiller. The dock extended a short distance into a river. Afraid the rototiller might slide into the water, I firmly gripped the handle. An unknown woman stood near me. I felt an urgent need to leave, and asked her to hold my rototiller. She stuck her foot out, and wedged it between a blade and the dock. As I let go of the handle, she grinned, and moved her foot. The rototiller tumbled into the water. I caught the handle, and sank to the bottom with it. The water was crystal clear. I saw all kinds of junk and debris. I firmly planted my feet, and shoved off the bottom with rototiller in tow. I shot through the surface of the water.

Mel Gibson was snorkeling, waiting for me. Seemingly aware of my situation, he grabbed the handle, smiled at me, and said, "I got it." **End of dream.**

Interpretation of dream: When something's "docked," like a boat, it's held up, or not used. The red rototiller indicates ministry. Red is the color of blood, and designates sacrifice. Rototillers plow soil. They're worthless sitting on a dock, or in water. In scripture, evil is occasionally personified as a woman. [Revelation 17:1-6] Like a seductress, evil entices and deceives.

If a thug or gangster said, "You're going to end up in the river," I'd know exactly what he meant; someone's going to die, and disappear. Garbage sits at the bottom of a river. Even the fish that swim there are known as scavengers or bottom feeders.

Mel Gibson is an Oscar winning actor and director. His films consistently pit underdogs against overwhelming odds. Without exception, the long-shot wins.

Here's what God was saying to me. My calling of preparing hearts for the Lord was docked, or held up. I even wanted to walk away. Evil sank me, and made me disappear. I found myself with the discards and dregs of society. Like a Mel Gibson character though, I rose and resurfaced.

I'm an overcomer.

Thank you, and blessings.

BIBLIOGRAPHY

Bickle, Mike. Song of Songs. International House of Prayer, 7542, 2003.

Blunt, James. "Cry." Back To Bedlam. Atlantic, 2005.

Demian, David. Conversation in Spring, 1998. Moncton, NB, Canada.

Fenn, John. Course Lecture. Destiny Training Center. Oakurst, CA. November, 2005.

The Flip Wilson Show. Writ. George Carlin and Don Hinkley. Dir. Bob Henry and Tim Kiley. Bob Henry Productions, 1970-1974.

Forbush, William Byron, Ed. Fox's Book of Martyrs. Grand Rapids, MI: Zondervan Publishing House, 1967.

Gladwell, Malcolm. The Tipping Point. New York: Little, Brown and Company, 2002. Pgs. 179-192.

Goodell, Gary. Mentoring Talk. Visalia, CA. February, 2006.

Jackson, J.B. A Dictionary of Scripture Proper Names. Neptune, New Jersey: Loizeaux Brothers, 1987.

Joyner, Rick. There Were Two Trees In The Garden. Charlotte NC: Morningstar Publ, 1992. Pg. 10.

Kaku, Michio. Parallel Worlds. New York: Anchor Books, February 2006. Pgs. 199, 219, 221.

Kierkegaard, Soren. Either/Or. Ed. Victor Eremita. Trans. Alastair Hannay. London: Penguin Books 2004. Pg. 20-21.

Mayer, John. "Bigger Than My Body." Heavier Things. Columbia, 2003.

Mills, Dick. Conversation in September, 1996. Moncton, NB, Canada.

Moore, John. Conversation in October, 2006. Miles City, Montana.

Morrison, Van. "Tupelo Honey." Tupelo Honey. Warner Brothers Records, 1971.

Nash, Johnny. "I Can See Clearly Now." I Can See Clearly Now. Epic, 1972.

New International Version Study Bible: 10th Anniversary Edition. Ed. Kenneth Barker. Grand Rapids, MI: Zondervan Publishing House, 1995.

Nietzsche, Friedrich. The Will To Power. Ed. Walter Kaufmann. Trans. Walter Kaufmann and R.J. Hollingdale. New York: Vintage Books, 1968. Pg. 417.

Ogle, Richard. Smart World. Boston: Harvard Business School Press, 2007. Pgs. 80-81.

______________________. Maintenance. New York: William Morrow & Company, Inc., 1974.

Polanyi, Michael. Personal Knowledge. Chicago: University of Chicago Press, 1962. Pgs. 394-405.

Santana. "Winning." Zebop. Columbia, 1981.

Springsteen, Bruce. "Badlands." Darkness On The Edge of Town. Columbia, 1978.

Stone, Joss. "Right To Be Wrong." Mind, Body, & Soul. EMI, 2004.

Storm, D. Anthony. D. Anthony Storm's Commentary On Kierkegaard. Available at http://www.sorenkierkegaard.org. Accessed 2008, 07-17.

Surowiecki, James. The Wisdom of Crowds. New York: Doubleday, June 2004. Pgs. XX-XXI.

Young's Literal Translation. 19 July 2008. http://www.searchgodsword.org

www.ingramcontent.com/pod-product-compliance
Lightning Source LLC
La Vergne TN
LVHW090947080826

845145LV00003B/916
9780976576402